Confession of Sin

Confession of Sin

by
John MacArthur, Jr.

Barry Clark
213 6309

MOODY PRESS
CHICAGO

Library of Congress Cataloging-in-Publication Data

MacArthur, John F.
   Confession of sin.

   (John MacArthur's Bible studies)
    1. Repentance — Biblical teaching. 2. Confession —
Biblical teaching. 3. Forgiveness of sin — Biblical
teaching. I. Title. II. Series: MacArthur, John F.
Bible studies.
BS680.R36M33   1986   241.3   85-32074
ISBN 0-8024-5093-8 (pbk.)

1 2 3 4 5 6 7 Printing/GB/Year 90 89 88 87 86

Printed in the United States of America

Contents

1
The Word of Life

Outline

Introduction
A. The Uncertainties
   1. In the world
   2. In the church
B. The Certainties
   1. Of Christianity
   2. Of Christ

Lesson
I. The Gospel Message Is Stable
   A. Abiding by True Teaching
   B. Avoiding False Teaching
      1. The warning from Jude
      2. The warning from Paul
      3. The warning from Peter
II. The Gospel Message Is Sensible
   A. We Have Heard
   B. We Have Seen
   C. We Have Looked Upon
   D. Our Hands Have Handled
III. The Gospel Message Is to Be Shared
IV. The Gospel Message Is the Source of Fellowship
   A. The Definition of Fellowship
      1. Supported by an Inscription
      2. Supported by Scripture
         a) 1 Corinthians 1:9
         b) Philippians 1:3-6
         c) 1 Peter 5:1
         d) 2 Peter 1:4
         e) 1 Corinthians 6:17
         f) Hebrews 2:11
   B. The Definition of Eternal Life
      1. Eternal life is spiritual life

2. Eternal life is resurrection life
3. Eternal life is endless life
4. Eternal life is abundant life

V. The Gospel Message Is the Supplier of Joy
   A. The Call to Joy
   B. The Cause of Joy
   C. The Clarification About Joy

Introduction

A. The Uncertainties

1. In the world

We live in a very uncertain day. The weight of insecurity has been laid on us from almost every angle imaginable. There is political and economic insecurity everywhere. Many parents are facing educational insecurity—they really don't know what their children are learning. We even have religious insecurity. Christianity has veered far from its foundations. We have slowly seen absolutes traded for opinions and dogmatism replaced by agnosticism. Absolutes are now mocked, and free thought has become revered. We hear the words *insecurity, change,* and *uncertainty* every day.

2. In the church

The church has followed Satan's leading to help build an insecure world. It has jumped on the bandwagon and replaced its absolutes with relatives and its truths with falsehoods. The church is confused and uncertain. It is asking itself what is right, what is important, and what is true. The book of 1 John is apropos for us because it is all about certainties. The apostle John dealt with dogmatism and absolutes in his epistle—not opinions.

B. The Certainties

1. Of Christianity

Christianity from its beginning was based on absolutes. Since then, those truths have been undermined by false teachers who have introduced uncertainties, insecurities, and changing doctrine. John wrote his three epistles to counteract the uncertainties that were being pushed onto Christians and Christianity. First John is a confident, absolute letter. There isn't much room for discussion about what John says. In fact, two Greek verbs for the

2

word *know* appear in that epistle thirty-six times. The characteristic noun of 1 John is the Greek word *parrhēsia*, which means "confidence" or "boldness." First John is about being bold on the basis of what you know.

There are basically three certainties that John deals with in his first epistle: the certainty of Jesus Christ, the certainty of obedience to the commandments of God, and the certainty of love for the brethren. John tells us what those certainties produce. He also states three reasons for writing the epistle. First he says in chapter 1, "These things write we unto you, that your joy may be full" (v. 4). Second he says, "These things write I unto you, that ye sin not" (2:1). And third he says, "These things have I written unto you that believe on the name of the Son of God, that ye may know that ye have eternal life" (5:13). First John was written so that your joy might be full, so that you would not sin, and so that you would be confident of your salvation.

For those purposes to be fulfilled, you need to know the certainties regarding the person of Christ, obedience to God's Word, and loving your brother. The result will be fellowship, holiness, and assurance. Belief in Christ results in obedience, and that produces love for the brethren. So, the three things John wants us to know—the proper view of Christ, obedience, and love—are the theme of his epistle.

2. Of Christ

The first thing John wants us to have is a proper belief in Christ. No one can become a Christian or say, "I know God," unless he has a proper Christology. John began his epistle by establishing who Christ is and then repeatedly stated that Christ has been verified as the Son of God. There are three ways to know that. The first is the historical event. First John 1:2 says, "The life was manifested." The second verification comes from apostolic testimony: "That which we have seen and heard declare we unto you" (v. 3). We have proof of who Christ is from His manifestation on earth and from the testimony of those who saw Him. The third corroborating testimony on who Christ is comes from the witness of the Spirit. First John 2 says, "Ye have an unction from the Holy One, and ye know all things. . . . The anointing which ye have received of him abideth in you" (vv. 20, 27). Who is

3

it that abides in us? The Holy Spirit. He teaches us all things.

The basic certainty of Christianity is that Jesus Christ is God in human flesh and that He is the Savior of the world. A man may say he is saved and that he walks in the light, but he must have a proper belief in Christ as the Son of God for that to be true. The three things verifying the certainty of Christ as God are the manifestation of Christ on earth, the testimony of the apostles, and the internal witness of the Holy Spirit. John talks about the certainty of Christ in the first four verses of his epistle: "That which was from the beginning, which we have heard, which we have seen with our eyes, which we have looked upon, and our hands have handled, of the Word of Life (For the life was manifested, and we have seen it, and bear witness, and show unto you that eternal life, which was with the Father, and was manifested unto us)—that which we have seen and heard declare we unto you, that ye also may have fellowship with us; and truly our fellowship is with the Father, and with his Son, Jesus Christ. And these things write we unto you, that your joy may be full."

In dealing with the certainty of Christ, John gives us five great certainties about "the Word of life" (1 John 1:1).

What is "the Word of life"?

The Greek text here literally reads, "the word of *the* life" (emphasis added). If you have the Authorized or *New American Standard* versions of the Bible, you will notice that the letter *w* in that phrase is capitalized. That's because the people who did those particular translations believed that "the word of life" referred to Jesus Christ. Many commentators compare 1 John 1:1 with John 1:1, which says, "In the beginning was the Word, and the Word was with God, and the Word was God." I accepted that for a while, but when I studied 1 John 1:1 in greater detail, I learned that "the word of the life" does not refer to Jesus Christ. You have to examine the original language in context to discover that. But we can't talk about the five certainties about the word of the life until you know what that is referring to.

You say, "Doesn't that phrase refer to Christ? There is a capital *w* there." That doesn't prove anything. Let me explain.

1. Verse 1 says, "That which was from the beginning, which we have heard, which we have seen with our eyes, which we have looked upon." The word *which* is in the neuter form. It seems to me that if John were referring to Christ he would have used the masculine form *He who* and not *which*.

2. If the main subject of verse 1 was "word," then verse 2 would say, "For the Word was manifested," instead of, "For the life was

4

manifested." Since "word" is ignored immediately after it is mentioned, it seems to me that the main subject of verse 1 is not "word" but "life." If the phrase "the life" in the Greek text refers to Jesus Christ (v. 2), then the word of the life refers to the message about Christ. John is not talking specifically about Christ Himself but about the gospel.

3. Verses 1 and 3 say, "That which was from the beginning, which we have heard . . . that which we have seen and heard declare we unto you, that ye also may have fellowship with us; and truly our fellowship is with the Father, and with his Son, Jesus Christ." Notice that we are not introduced to Christ until the end of verse 3. If John had been talking about Christ all along, starting with the phrase "the word of life" in verse 1, he would have ended verse 3 by saying, "our fellowship is with the Father, and with the Word," not "and with his Son." The first mention of Christ comes at the end of verse 3, apart from the parenthesis in verse 2.

4. Verse 1 begins, "That which was from the beginning." Some people say that is a reference to the preincarnate existence of Christ—that "the Word of life" existed before the world began. It's true Christ existed prior to the incarnation, but that's not what John is talking about here. The phrase "from the beginning" does not refer to eternity; it refers to the beginning of preaching the gospel. That same phrase is used in 1 John 2:7: "Brethren, I write no new commandment unto you, but an old commandment which ye had from the beginning." John is referring to the first time his audience heard the gospel message. First John 2:24 uses that phrase again: "If that which ye have heard from the beginning shall remain in you." The prepositional phrase in all three of the above verses refers to when people first heard the gospel message.

You say, "Wait a minute. First John 2:13 says, 'I write unto you, fathers, because ye have known him that is from the beginning.' The apostle obviously used the phrase *from the beginning* in that verse in reference to God."

5. The construction of the Greek text in 1 John 1:1 is different from the construction that appears in 2:13. First John 2:13 has a definite article (Gk., *ton aparchēs*), which renders it "the One from the beginning." When God wanted the phrase "from the beginning" to speak of eternity, He said *ton aparchēs*. But when He wanted to say, "From the beginning of preaching," He dropped the definite article and just said *aparchēs*.

5

So John is saying, "I am going to tell you about the word of the life: the gospel message."

Let's look at five certainties regarding the word of the life.

Lesson

I. THE GOSPEL MESSAGE IS STABLE

A. Abiding by True Teaching

The epistle begins, "That which was from the beginning . . . of the Word of life . . . declare we unto you" (vv. 1, 3). Remember, John wasn't talking about Christ and eternity; he was referring to the good news and the beginning of its proclamation. He was saying, "We are telling you the same message that has been proclaimed from the very beginning of preaching. Let's get back to basic truth."

B. Avoiding False Teaching

The people John was writing to (who were most likely in Asia Minor) had been exposed to the truth of the gospel. Not long afterward, Satan moved in with false teachers and started drawing people away from the truth. Those false teachers were gnostics. The docetic gnostics said Christ was a phantom. The Cerinthian gnostics said that the Christ spirit came upon Jesus at His baptism and departed just before He died on the cross. The gnostics were trying to introduce new theology into the church. John was saying, "Go back to what you learned when you first heard the gospel message."

The hymn "Wonderful Words of Life" says, "Sing them over again to me, wonderful words of life." "Tell me the old, old story," says the hymn by the same name. I don't want a new message, do you? But that's what false teachers offer. John was saying, "Don't take up something new; stick with what was proclaimed from the beginning." When anyone teaches a new doctrine or revelation, hang onto the original message. Any new teachings are heresy. When someone comes along with something new, I don't want it; I want the same message that has been preached since the gospel was first proclaimed. What a beautiful way for John to begin his epistle! From the onset he crushes the doctrines the gnostics were teaching: "That which was from the beginning . . . of the Word of life . . . declare we unto you" (vv. 1, 3).

1. The warning from Jude

Look at Jude 3-4: "Beloved, when I gave all diligence to

6

write unto you of the common salvation, it was needful for me to write unto you, and exhort you that ye should earnestly contend for the faith which was once delivered unto the saints. For there are certain men crept in unawares, who were before of old ordained to this condemnation, ungodly men, turning the grace of our God into lasciviousness, and denying the only Lord God, and our Lord Jesus Christ." Jude was saying, "I have to remind you to fight for the faith that was once delivered to the saints because there are people who want to add to it." The word *once* near the end of verse 3 is the Greek word *hapax*, which means "once for all." The faith—that is, the gospel—was delivered once for all. It is stable and will always be the same. There will never be another gospel or faith. There will never be new visions or anything else that adulterates the gospel. Hebrews 13:8 says, "Jesus Christ [is] the same yesterday, and today, and forever."

2. The warning from Paul

The Galatians also had to deal with false teachers. After Paul had preached the gospel to them, Judaizers came with what they considered to be extended revelation. They were saying, "We need to tell the Galatians everything. Paul didn't tell them all the truth because he didn't want to offend people." Paul told the Galatians, "I marvel that ye are so soon removed from him that called you into the grace of Christ unto another gospel, which is not another; but there are some that trouble you, and would pervert the gospel of Christ. But though we, or an angel from heaven, preach any other gospel . . . let him be accursed" (1:6-8). There is no place for anything but the true gospel.

In Galatians 2:5 Paul says, "To [false teachers] we gave place by subjection, no, not for an hour, that the truth of the gospel might continue with you." We are not to listen to false teachers at all that the truth of the gospel might remain with us. Paul told the Corinthians, "I delivered unto you first of all that which I also received, that Christ died for our sins according to the scriptures; and that he was buried, and that he rose again the third day according to the scriptures" (1 Cor. 15:3-4). He was saying, "That's the gospel message I delivered to you from God, and it has not changed."

7

3. The warning from Peter

Peter wrote these words: "This second epistle, beloved, I now write unto you, in both of which I stir up your pure minds by way of remembrance" (2 Pet. 3:1). Peter wasn't going to teach something new; he wanted to remind people of what they already knew so that they might "be mindful of the words which were spoken before by the holy prophets, and of the commandment of the apostles of the Lord and Savior" (v. 2). He was simply reminding people of the truths they already knew concerning Christ.

One of the great certainties of Christianity is that it does not change. There are no new revelations; there is no new gospel.

II. THE GOSPEL MESSAGE IS SENSIBLE

John experienced the gospel with his senses. He rejected heresy about Christ because he knew the gospel was unchanging and because he had experienced the word of the life. First John 1 begins, "That which was from the beginning, which we have heard, which we have seen with our eyes, which we have looked upon, and our hands have handled, of the Word of life . . . declare we unto you" (vv. 1, 3). He was saying, "You can take my word about the certitude of the gospel because I have experienced it, heard it, seen it, looked at it, and handled it." You say, "How can you handle the word of the life? How can you see and touch it? How could John say he had experienced it?"

The answer is in verse 2: "The life was manifested [Gk., *phaneroō*], and we have seen it, and bear witness, and show unto you that eternal life, which was with the Father, and was manifested unto us." John experienced the word of the life because it was personified. John 1:14 says, "The Word was made flesh, and dwelt among us (and we beheld his glory, the glory as of the only begotten of the Father), full of grace and truth." The truth was incarnate; Christ was manifest in human flesh. John was saying, "No heretic can sway me because I have experienced the manifestation of the life, which is Jesus Christ."

Let's look at how John perceived the word of the life, as stated in verse 1. Notice as we go along there is a deepening intimacy in the perceptions.

A. We Have Heard

The verb in the phrase *we have heard* is in the perfect tense, which indicates an action completed in the past that has

8

present results. John was saying, in effect, "We heard repeatedly." And after he heard Christ, his words were still producing results. That's interesting because the epistle was written around A.D. 90, and John is looking back to when he was with Christ about sixty years earlier. What John had heard was still having an impact on his life. That's an illustration of the perfect tense: something completed in the past that still has present results.

Just think about what the apostles had heard when they were with Christ. John had been close to Christ; he had leaned on Christ's breast during the Last Supper (John 13:25). And here in 1 John he is saying, "Sixty years later, I'm still living on the thrills I got from what I heard!"

B. We Have Seen

Verse 1 says, "We have seen with our eyes." He said that so his readers would know he wasn't referring to spiritual sight. The Greek word *horaō*, which means "to see," refers to physical sight. He saw Jesus Christ with his own eyes. That was important for him to say because the docetic gnostics taught that Jesus Christ was a phantom. John shot that teaching to pieces.

John used the perfect tense here too. He saw Christ for a long time, and sixty years later he was still confident that what he saw was true. He saw Christ do miracles that were divine in origin.

C. We Have Looked Upon

The Greek word for "looked upon" is *theaomai*, which means "to gaze long." John was not talking about a passing glance, but a steadfast, searching gaze. The apostles penetrated the life of Christ. They had examined Him as closely as they could, watching Him day in and day out. For three years they saw Him in many situations. The longer they watched Him, the more convinced they were about who He was.

D. Our Hands Have Handled

This is the epitome of John's perception. The Greek word translated "handled" is *epsēlaphēsan*. The same Greek word is used in the Septuagint in Genesis 27, when blind Isaac felt Jacob's hands and thought it was Esau, Jacob's brother (vv. 22-23). That word is used to speak of a blind man groping or feeling for something. Another form of that word is used in Luke 24:39; Jesus says to those with Him on the road to

9

Emmaus, "Handle me, and see." In John 20:27, Christ tells Thomas, "Reach here thy hand, and thrust it into my side." So, the disciples had literally touched Christ. John had touched Him when he had "leaned on his breast at supper" (John 21:20).

So the message John was declaring had to do with the word of the life. "The Word" simply refers to the message about the life, who is Christ. In 1 John 1:2 he says, "The life was manifested, and we have seen it, and bear witness, and show unto you that eternal life, which was with the Father, and was manifested unto us." The fact that Christ was with the Father in eternity is indicated there. How did the disciples know about the divine life? It was manifest in human flesh.

III. THE GOSPEL MESSAGE IS TO BE SHARED

The word of life is to be shared. Two key words point that out. One is in verse 2: "For the life was manifested, and we have seen it, and bear witness, and show unto you that eternal life." The word for "bear witness" (Gk., *marturomai*) is also the root of our English word *martyr*. It means "to give a personal testimony." John was saying, "This is something that we share with you." The second key word appears in verse 3: "That which we have seen and heard declare we unto you." The word "declare" (Gk., *apangellō*) means "to proclaim doctrine." John was telling his readers, "We have shared the gospel with you by personal testimony and by proclaiming doctrine." That's how we witness: We present the gospel of the Lord Jesus Christ, and we share what God has done for us. So in essence John said, "What was a manifestation to us has become a proclamation to you. We have shared with you from personal experience and doctrine."

Our personal witness and proclamation are both parts of evangelism. Second Peter 1:15-16 says, "I will endeavor that ye may be able, after my decease, to have these things always in remembrance. For we have not followed cunningly devised fables when we made known unto you the power and coming of our Lord Jesus Christ, but were eyewitnesses of his majesty." Peter spoke from personal experience. Then in verse 19 he says, "We have also a more sure word of prophecy." Thus, Peter declared things from the standpoint of revelation in addition to speaking from personal experience.

Christ manifested Himself to the disciples, and they became responsible to propagate what they had heard. One of the certainties of the gospel message is that it is to be shared. We are to witness to others and proclaim Christ's message. Even though we are not apostles, Christ has manifested Himself to us. First Peter 1:8 says, "Whom, having not seen, ye love." In Acts 1:8, Christ tells the apostles that the Holy Spirit will come upon them and that they will be witnesses of Him. Second Corinthians 5:19-20 says we have been called to be ambassadors and have been given the ministry of reconciliation. The gospel message is stable and unchanging. It is sensible and perceivable. And it is to be shared by way of personal testimony as well as doctrinal proclamation.

IV. THE GOSPEL MESSAGE IS THE SOURCE OF FELLOWSHIP

Why all this proclamation? Why all this mention of experience? John gives the answer in verse 3: "That which we have seen and heard declare we unto you, that ye also may have fellowship with us; and truly our fellowship is with the Father, and with his Son, Jesus Christ." The purpose of proclaiming the gospel is to create a fellowship. The proclamation of the gospel is not an end in itself.

A. The Definition of Fellowship

The word "fellowship" in verse 3 is an extremely important word; it is commonly used in Christian circles. The Greek word, *koinōnia*, is translated "communion," and in the noun form, it is translated "partner" or "partaker." However, what we think of fellowship today is different from what people thought of it back then. We think of it in terms of social relationships: person-to-person contact. But that's not the meaning of the word in 1 John 1:3. *Koinōnia* refers to a person having joint participation with another person in a common possession. The literal meaning of the word is "partnership." *Koinōnia* does not refer to social interaction but to absolute union in a common thing.

1. Supported by an inscription

Archaeologists have found a fourth-century inscription that was written by a doctor to his wife, who also studied medicine. He wrote, "With you alone I have shared my life." In that extrabiblical inscription, the Greek word for *shared* is *koinōnia*. The doctor was referring to his marriage. So, *koinōnia* referred to a partnership. It was used synonymously with marriage. It's true there are social implications in marriage, but the true meaning of *koinōnia* had less to do with the social relationship than with the actual partnership involved.

11

2. Supported by Scripture

John wouldn't have been referring to social relationships when he wrote 1 John 1:3 because it was impossible for him to have met with all the people he was writing to (1 John is a general epistle written to a general audience). Therefore, *fellowship* would not have referred to some kind of social relationship, such as ministering spiritual gifts to one another. Nor was he talking about a mystical companionship with the Lord. Some Greek scholars say that the Greek word translated "with us" (*meta*) together with the verb *have* refers to partnership. So, John was saying, "We have declared the message of eternal life so that you might become partners with us in the same eternal life." John wasn't inviting the readers of his letter to a fellowship hall; he was inviting them to be saved. He wasn't after cookies and punch; he wanted them to believe in Christ! He wanted them to have fellowship with the Father and the Son and to have eternal life. There are other passages that support what John was talking about.

a) 1 Corinthians 1:9

Paul said, "God is faithful, by whom ye were called unto the fellowship of his son, Jesus Christ our Lord." Keep in mind that the Corinthian church had many problems. Several of the people in it had sinned publicly. If fellowship had referred to socializing, Paul would have said, "You are out of fellowship," because sinning Christians are to be put out of the church until they repent of what they are doing. But fellowship refers to the believer's union with Christ: Christians are "called unto the fellowship of [God's] Son, Jesus Christ." Every believer is a partaker of eternal life, even though he may sin from time to time.

You'll notice that 1 John 1:3 says, "Our fellowship is with the Father, and with his Son, Jesus Christ." You say, "What about the Holy Spirit?" Paul talked about the fellowship of the Holy Spirit in 2 Corinthians 13:14. The Holy Spirit, as a member of the Trinity, is included in our fellowship.

b) Philippians 1:3-6

In verses 3-5 Paul says, "I thank my God upon every remembrance of you, always in every prayer of mine

12

for you all making request with joy, for your fellowship in the gospel from the first day until now." What first day was Paul talking about? He was referring to the Philippians' fellowship "in the gospel," which began from the time they were saved. Fellowship starts when you're saved and goes on forever. Paul wasn't referring to having a great get-together with the Philippians from the time they were converted. That would have been impossible because he was always traveling. In fact, he wrote the letter to the Philippians from a jail cell in Rome. He certainly wasn't socializing with them from there. When he said "fellowship," he was referring to their partnership in eternal life.

Paul continues in verse 6, "Being confident of this very thing, that he who hath begun a good work in you will perform it until the day of Jesus Christ." God began His "good work" in the Philippians when He put them into the fellowship. In effect, Paul was saying, "I know you will stay in the fellowship until Christ returns because it's His business to keep you there."

c) 1 Peter 5:1

Peter said, "The elders who are among you I exhort, who am also an elder, and a witness of the sufferings of Christ, and also a partaker [Gk., koinōnos] of the glory that shall be revealed." The word "partaker" is a positional word; Peter was saying he was a partner in eternal glory.

d) 2 Peter 1:4

Here the apostle wrote, "[You have received] exceedingly great and precious promises, that by these ye might be partakers [Gk., koinōnoi] of the divine nature." Being in the fellowship is the same thing as being saved. All Christians are in the fellowship. Don't let someone come up to you and say, "You're out of the fellowship," because that would be the same as saying, "You have lost your salvation." For the believer, there is an eternal, inviolable sharing in the life of the Trinity. It is astounding to realize that the eternal life of God dwells within us forever. Nothing can violate our eternal character.

13

e) 1 Corinthians 6:17

Here Paul said, "He that is joined unto the Lord is one spirit." He said that because we share common eternal life—Christ's life is our life.

f) Hebrews 2:11

According to this passage, Jesus is not ashamed to call us His brothers. We bear the same life He bears.

Since I have the same life Christ does, I'm never out of the fellowship. You say, "Are you saying you're perfect?" No, I'm merely saying we will never be out of the fellowship because it's a partnership in eternal life. You ask, "What exactly is eternal life?"

B. The Definition of Eternal Life

1. Eternal life is spiritual life

The life we have received because Christ dwells in us is spiritual life, not physical life. In John 5:25 Christ says, "I say unto you, The hour is coming, and now is, when the dead shall hear the voice of the Son of God; and they that hear shall live." He was saying, "The gospel is now being preached and spiritually dead men are coming alive." Ephesians 2:1 says that we who were dead in sin have been made alive by Christ. We have been given spiritual life. What is spiritual life? Sensitivity to God. When a person becomes a believer, he suddenly becomes conscious of God. A person who is spiritually alive is like someone who is physically alive, and someone who is spiritually dead is like a corpse that cannot respond to physical stimulus. When God pricks a spiritually dead man, nothing happens. But a person who is spiritually alive responds to God.

2. Eternal life is resurrection life

Someday, we are going to rise up from the grave. When we die, our spirits will go to be with Christ, and our bodies will one day join our spirits (1 Cor. 15:51-53; 2 Cor. 5:8).

3. Eternal life is endless life

How long will we live? Forever.

4. Eternal life is abundant life

Christ says in John 10:10, "I am come that they might have life, and that they might have it more abundantly."

We have abundant life.

Eternal life is spiritual life, resurrection life, endless life, and abundant life. That is certain.

The word of life is stable. It meets the need of every man. It is sensible and is shared by testimony and proclamation. "The Word of life" is the source of fellowship. That fellowship is a partnership in eternal life.

V. THE GOSPEL MESSAGE IS THE SUPPLIER OF JOY

A. The Call to Joy

One of the great certainties about the word of the life is that it gives joy. First John 1:4 says, "And these things write we unto you, that your joy may be full." The word "and" at the beginning of the verse is the Greek word *kai*, which is a connective and can have many different meanings. I looked at the text for a while trying to figure out how it could best be interpreted. It probably could be best translated "in addition to." In that case, John would be saying, "In addition to all I have already written, I write that your joy might be full." It is possible to be a Christian and not have full joy. John was writing his letter to the members of the fellowship so that they might enjoy the fullness of all they had in Christ. In addition to wanting those people to be in the fellowship, he wanted them to know the full joy of the fellowship.

In some manuscripts, verse 4 reads, "These things write we unto you, that *your* joy may be full" (emphasis added). Other manuscripts read, "These things write we unto you, that *our* joy may be full" (emphasis added). B. F. Westcott says, "Both readings . . . are well supported and both give good sense" (*The Epistles of St. John* [Grand Rapids: Eerdmans, 1966], p. 13). Let's assume John used the word *our* because it would encompass everyone described by the word *your*. (I'm sure that John didn't want to be unhappy!) Therefore, he's saying, "I want us all to have full joy in this fellowship." A Christian can be really miserable. Some believers don't have full joy. John didn't write his epistle just to get people saved; he wanted to tell other believers that in addition to being in the fellowship and having eternal life, God intended for them to have full joy.

B. The Cause of Joy

In 2 John 4, John writes, "I rejoiced greatly that I found . . . thy children walking in truth." John wanted all believers to have full joy. Do you know what gave him joy? He rejoiced when the readers of his letter were walking in the truth. In verse 12 he continues, "Having many things to write unto you, I would not write with paper and ink, but I trust to come unto you, and speak face-to-face, that our joy may be full." There John said *"our* joy," as we assume he did in 1 John 1:4. In 3 John 4, the apostle writes, "I have no greater joy than to hear that my children walk in truth." John was saying in his first epistle, "Let's all be happy. If you do what I tell you, you'll have joy—and I will rejoice from seeing you do those things."

C. The Clarification About Joy

Do you know what joy is? It's full satisfaction. If you are a Christian, you should be absolutely satisfied. If you don't have joy, you are admitting that the salvation God has accomplished isn't satisfactory. The proclamation of the gospel creates fellowship, and the fellowship creates joy. Jesus wants us to have joy (John 15:11; 16:24; 17:13). He wants our joy to be full. Paul told the Philippians, "Rejoice in the Lord always; and again I say, Rejoice" (4:4). The words *rejoice* and *rejoicing* appear about seventy times in the New Testament. Christians ought to be people who are fully satisfied.

The theme of 1 John is that there are three great certainties: the person of Christ, obedience to God, and love for the brethren. One of the by-products of those certainties is full joy. John wrote his epistle so you might have full joy. If you don't, it's because you aren't applying to your life the three certainties he wrote about. There are five great certainties about the word of life: It is stable, it is personally experienced, it is to be shared with others, it is the source of fellowship, and it is the source of joy.

Focusing on the Facts

1. What has Christianity been based on since its beginning? What have false teachers done since (see p. 2)?

2. What are the three certainties John deals with in his first epistle (see p. 3)?

3. State the three reasons John wrote his first epistle (see p. 3).

4. How did John show that Christ had been verified as the Son of God (see p. 3)?

5. Explain why the phrase "the word of life" in 1 John 1:1 does not refer to Christ (see pp. 4-5).

6. What did John mean when he said, "That which was from the beginning . . . of the word of life . . . declare we unto you" (1 John 1:1, 3; see p. 5)?

7. What did the docetic gnostics say that Christ was? What did the Cerinthian gnostics teach about Him (see p. 6)?

8. What exhortation is given in Jude 3-4 (see pp. 6-7)?

9. What did Paul say should happen to anyone who teaches something other than the true gospel (Gal. 1:6-8; see p. 7)?

10. What was the basic message that Paul had given to the Corinthians (1 Cor. 15:3-4; see p. 7)?

11. John rejected heresy about Christ because he had experienced "the Word of life." Explain how he could say that (see p. 8).

12. In light of the phrases "we have heard" and "we have seen" in 1 John 1:1, what does the perfect tense in the Greek text indicate (see pp. 8-9)?

13. Why was it important for John to say that he saw Christ with his own eyes in 1 John 1:1 (see p. 9)?

14. Did the apostles get only a glimpse of Christ's life? Explain (see p. 9).

15. What was the epitome of John's perception of Christ, as expressed in 1 John 1:1 (see p. 9)?

16. What two key words in 1 John 1:2-3 point out that "the Word of life" is to be shared? What do those words mean (see p. 10)?

17. What did the disciples become responsible for after Christ manifested Himself to them? Do we have the same responsibility? Support your answer with Scripture (see p. 10).

18. According to 1 John 1:3, what is the purpose of proclaiming the gospel (see p. 11)?

19. What meaning do people frequently give to the word *fellowship* today? What does the word fellowship in 1 John 1:3 mean (see p. 11)?

20. Discuss the biblical definition of *fellowship* (see p. 12).

21. Give the definition of eternal life (see p. 12).

22. According to 1 John 1:4, what does the gospel message supply (see p. 14)?

23. What gave John joy? Support your answer with Scripture (see pp. 15-16).

24. What is joy (see p. 16)?

Pondering the Principles

1. One thing the apostle John discussed in his first epistle is proper belief in Christ. A person must understand certain things about Christ before he can become a Christian. Write your answers to the following questions: Who is Christ (see Isaiah 9:6; Micah 5:2; Matthew 1:23; John 1:1)? Why did Christ come to earth (see Matthew 5:17-18; 20:28; Luke 4:18-19; John 3:16-17)? Why did He die on the cross (see 1 Cor. 15:3; 2 Cor. 5:18-19, 21)? Using what you have just learned, how would you explain to someone who Christ is and what He did on earth?

2. The gospel is unchanging. Paul said in Galatians 1:8, "Though we, or an angel from heaven, should preach to you a gospel contrary to that which we have preached to you, let him be accursed" (NASB)[1]. To find out more about the certainty of the gospel, answer the following: What did Christ say about the Old Testament (Luke 16:17)? What do we find out about the Word of God from 2 Timothy 3:16-17 and 2 Peter 1:19-21? What do we find out about the nature of Scripture in Isaiah 40:8 and Psalm 19:7? Meditate on Psalm 19:7-11 and discuss why it is so important for all believers to know the Bible.

3. The apostles experienced Christ firsthand; they interacted with Him for about three years. Therefore, they would be the most qualified persons to tell us about Him. Since we are studying from John's first epistle, let's take the opportunity to read what John wrote about Christ elsewhere. Carefully read John 1:1-14 and 3:31-36 and write down everything you learn about Christ from those passages. Each day this week, meditate on what you wrote and let those truths become ingrained in your mind and heart.

---

*New American Standard Bible.

2
If We Confess Our Sins—
Part 1

Outline

Introduction
A. Great Words from Men
B. Great Words from the Bible
  1. The necessity of admitting sin
  2. The practice of denying sin
    a) In Malachi
    b) In 1 John

Lesson
I. The Declaration
  A. Articulating the Definitions of Light and Darkness
    1. The intellectual aspect
    2. The moral aspect
  B. Applying the Definitions of Light and Darkness
    1. To God
    2. To people
II. The Distinction
  A. Those Who Say They Are Christians
    1. The clarification
    2. The claims
      a) Expressed
      b) Examined
        (1) Darkness
          (a) The refutation of the claim
          (b) The requirement for obedience
        (2) Deceit
          (a) Denying the reality of sin
          (b) Declaring the reality of sin
        (3) Defamation

Introduction

A. Great Words from Men

Every civilization in history has developed certain sayings that people quote frequently. We ourselves say things like "Too many cooks spoil the broth" and "A bird in the hand is worth two in the bush." Beyond that, there are great and significant statements. History books tell us Patrick Henry's famous words, "Give me liberty, or give me death!" If we study literature, we read these words from Shakespeare: "To be, or not to be: that is the question" (*Hamlet*, III.i.56) and "To thine own self be true" (I.iii.78). From early philosophers we get "Know thyself" (an inscription on the temple of Apollo at Delphi; Plato, *Protagoras*, 343b, ascribes the saying to the Seven Wise Men). People have a penchant for recording great sayings.

B. Great Words from the Bible

God has a penchant for great truths, and He has recorded those truths in the Bible. We should memorize them; they should become a part of us. Of all the profound truths that are recorded in Scripture, among the most important is:

1. The necessity of admitting sin

   a) Genesis 41:9—"Then spoke the chief butler unto Pharaoh, saying, I do remember my faults this day."

   b) Genesis 44:16—"Judah said [to Joseph], What shall we say unto my lord? What shall we speak? Or how shall we clear ourselves? God hath found out the iniquity of thy servants."

   c) Exodus 9:27—"Pharaoh sent, and called for Moses and Aaron, and said unto them, I have sinned this time; the Lord is righteous, and I and my people are wicked."

   d) Exodus 10:16—"Pharaoh called for Moses and Aaron in haste; and he said, I have sinned against the Lord your God."

   e) 1 Samuel 15:24—"Saul said unto Samuel, I have sinned; for I have transgressed the commandment of the Lord."

   f) 2 Samuel 12:13—"David said unto Nathan, I have sinned against the Lord."

g) 2 Samuel 24:10 —"David said unto the Lord, I have sinned greatly in what I have done . . . I have done very foolishly."

h) 1 Chronicles 21:17 —David said to God, "I it is who has sinned and done evil indeed."

i) Psalm 32:5 —"I acknowledged my sin unto thee, and mine iniquity have I not hidden."

j) Psalm 38:1-4 —"O Lord, rebuke me not in thy wrath; neither chasten me in thy hot displeasure. For thine arrows stick fast in me, and thy hand presseth me greatly. There is no soundness in my flesh because of thine anger; neither is there any rest in my bones because of my sin. For mine iniquities are gone over mine head; like an heavy burden they are too heavy for me."

k) Psalm 40:12—"Innumerable evils have compassed me about. Mine iniquities have taken hold upon me, so that I am not able to look up. They are more than the hairs of mine head; therefore, my heart faileth me."

l) Psalm 41:4 —"I said, Lord be merciful unto me, heal my soul; for I have sinned against thee."

m) Psalm 51:1—"Have mercy upon me, O God."

n) Isaiah 6:5 —The prophet Isaiah said, "Woe is me! For I am undone, because I am a man of unclean lips, and I dwell in the midst of a people of unclean lips."

o) Daniel 9:20 —Daniel said, "I was speaking, and praying, and confessing my sin."

p) Matthew 27:4 —After Judas betrayed Christ, he said, "I have sinned in that I have betrayed innocent blood."

q) Luke 5:8 —Peter said to Jesus, "Depart from me; for I am a sinful man, O Lord."

r) Luke 15:18 —"I will get up and go to my father, and will say to him, 'Father, I have sinned against heaven, and in your sight'" (NASB).

s) Luke 18:13 —"The tax collector . . . smote upon his breast, saying, God be merciful to me a sinner."

t) 1 Timothy 1:15—"It is a trustworthy statement,

deserving full acceptance, that Christ Jesus came into the world to save sinners, among whom I am foremost of all"(NASB).

Those statements are significant because they are acknowledgments of sin. Such acknowledgment is basic to glorifying God. In Joshua 7:19, Joshua said this to Achan, a man whose sin brought great disaster to all Israel: "My son, give, I pray thee, glory to the Lord God of Israel, and make confession unto him." It is always a profound thing for a person to acknowledge sin.

2. The practice of denying sin

Today it is not popular to admit you are a sinner, who has broken God's law. Men avoid the issue of sin or deny it. They call sin by other names in an effort to escape the ultimate end of sin, which is punishment. People know where there is sin, there will be retribution. Romans 1:32 tells us man is aware that there's a moral law and that there are consequences to it. The only way man can eliminate the fear of judgment in his mind is to ignore morality. Many people feel that if they ignore sin, hell will go away. Biblical standards have become a joke to the world. The Bible is accused of presenting an antiquated, narrow, objectionable morality that is out of touch with life and the times.

Some people think refusal to face sin is a new thing; they associate it with the advent of psychological explanations for everything in behavior. Psychologists often attribute sinfulness to what may have happened to you before you were born, things your parents may have done to you while you were growing up, or poor secretion of the endocrine glands as a result of stress. But denial of sin has been taking place throughout man's history. Men have been covering their sins for centuries in an effort to avoid facing their consequences. The law of morality is innate: It will be well for the good and bad for the evil (Prov. 19:23; Rom. 1:18-19). The only way men can escape their innate knowledge of judgment is by eliminating morality. Some deny their sins overtly or philosophically; others deny them experientially (they say sin doesn't exist, or they live like it doesn't). There are some illustrations of such denial.

a) In Malachi

(1) Malachi 2:1-4, 6

22

Here we read, "Now, O ye priests, this commandment is for you. If ye will not hear, and if ye will not lay it to heart, to give glory unto my name, saith the Lord of hosts, I will even send a curse upon you, and I will curse your blessings; yea, I have cursed them already, because ye do not lay it to heart. Behold, I will corrupt your seed, and spread dung upon your faces, even the dung of your solemn feasts; and one shall take you away with it. And ye shall know that I have sent this commandment unto you, that my covenant might be with Levi, saith the Lord of hosts." The Israelites were not admitting their sin, and God said He would judge them for that. They were saying, In what way have we sinned? (Mal. 1:6).

(2) Malachi 2:11-12, 14

In this passage, God talks about the people's marriage relationships: "Judah hath dealt treacherously, and an abomination is committed in Israel and in Jerusalem; for Judah hath profaned the holiness of the Lord which he loved, and hath married the daughter of a foreign god. The Lord will cut off the man that doeth this, the master and the scholar, out of the tabernacles of Jacob" (vv. 11-12). Verse 14 continues, "Yet ye say, Why? Because the Lord hath been witness between thee and the wife of thy youth, against whom thou hast dealt treacherously; yet is she thy companion, and the wife of thy covenant." God punishes violations of the marriage covenant.

(3) Malachi 3:8-9

God told the Israelites, "Will a man rob God? Yet ye have robbed me. But ye say, How have we robbed thee? In tithes and offerings" (v. 8). The people weren't paying taxes to their theocratic government. Verse 9 continues, "Ye are cursed with a curse; for ye have robbed me, even this whole nation." God cursed the Israelites as a result of what they had done.

(4) Malachi 3:2-3

23

Here we read there is coming One who will be like "a refiner's fire. . . . He shall sit like a refiner and purifier of silver; and he shall purify the sons of Levi, and purge them like gold and silver, that they may offer unto the Lord an offering in righteousness."

(5) Malachi 4:1

"For, behold, the day cometh, that shall burn like an oven, and all the proud, yea, and all that do wickedly, shall be stubble."

All the judgment God pronounced in the book of Malachi came to pass because the Israelites sinned and failed to recognize that. The recognition that man is a sinner is foundational to a relationship with God; consequently, Satan is busy propagating false doctrine about sin. He says that sin doesn't exist, it doesn't matter, or that God is so full of love He couldn't care less whether you sin or not. However, sin *does* matter, and John talks about that in his first epistle.

b) In 1 John

There have always been false teachers who deny sin, and there always will be. When John wrote his first epistle, people known as the gnostics (their title comes from the Greek word *gnosis*, which means "knowledge") were trying to influence the people John was writing to. They taught that Christ was not really a man and that the biblical revelation about Him was simply a fable. They said Christ had not really existed and was only a phantom who appeared to be human. The people who taught that were called Docetists, a title drawn from the Greek word *dokeō* , which means "to appear to be." Another group of gnostics, the Cerinthians, said Christ was a man. However, they attributed His qualities of deity to a Christ spirit that had descended upon Him at baptism and left Him shortly before His crucifixion. In addition to teaching heresy about Christ, the gnostics taught heresy concerning sin. According to them, matter was evil and spirit was good; therefore, anything you did in the flesh had no effect on your spirit. They thought your spirit could be godly no matter

24

what you did with your body; that was a very popular theology.

The gnostics did not confess sin. The Greek word for *confess* means "to say the same thing." The gnostics did not say the same thing about sin that God did, nor did they confess Christ. They were among those 1 John 4:3 warns us about. So the heresy of gnosticism was that it did not say the same thing that God said about Christ or sin.

In the first four verses of 1 John, the apostle talks about Christ. After that, he confronts the gnostics about sin. He says, in effect, "I don't care if they claim to be Christians and say they are in the fellowship. They aren't, because they don't say the same thing about sin that God does. A person has to know what God says about sin before he can come to a knowledge of the truth." There is a simple test you can apply to find out who is in the fellowship: Find out what a person's view of sin is. John gives two other tests later on in his first epistle: a person's obedience to God and his love for the brethren. The first test of whether someone is in the fellowship is his confession of Christ; the second test is his confession of sin. The third test is his obedience, and the fourth is his love. A man's verbal profession of Christ can't always be believed. According to the passages we will study in this lesson and the next, we can test a person by his perspective on sin. In 1 John 1:5, the apostle presents a basic premise and then draws the distinction between those who claim to be in the fellowship and those who really are, basing his distinction on their view of sin.

Lesson

I. THE DECLARATION (v. 5)

"This, then, is the message which we have heard of him, and declare unto you, that God is light, and in him is no darkness at all."

In verses 1-4, John lays the foundation of his epistle, the incarnation of Jesus Christ being the main point. When someone believes Jesus is God in human flesh and receives the work of Christ by faith, he enters into the fellowship. The Christian life, then, is fellowship with God. Notice verse 3 says we have fellowship with the Father, the Son, and each other. Since the Christian life is defined as being in the fellowship, not being in the fellowship is the same thing as not being a Christian. You can never say a Christian is out of the fellowship because being in the fellowship is synonymous with being saved. A believer's fellowship is with God, and he should know the basic character and nature of God. That becomes the foundation for the distinction between a true Christian and a false one.

First John 1:5 begins, "This, then, is the message which we have heard of him [God]." The message John was preaching was not human opinion; it was a revelation from God. It was divine truth. What was the message? Verse 5 continues, "God is light, and in him is no darkness at all." That is a tremendous absolute about the nature of God: He is light. (Later in the epistle, John also says that God is life [5:11-12, 20] and love [4:16]. There is no darkness in God.

A. Articulating the Definitions of Light and Darkness

Light and darkness are familiar symbols in Scripture. From the intellectual aspect, light refers to truth, and darkness refers to error or ignorance. From the moral aspect, darkness has to do with sin and evil, and light refers to holiness and purity. Let's look at some Scriptures that illustrate that.

1. The intellectual aspect

   a) Proverbs 6:23—"For the commandment is a lamp, and the law is light." The law of God is light; it is truth.

   b) Psalm 119:105—"Thy word is a lamp unto my feet, and a light unto my path."

   c) Psalm 119:130—"The entrance of thy words giveth light; it giveth understanding." In Scripture, the word *light* is often used to speak of the truth and the comprehension of it.

   d) John 1:4—"In him was life; and the life was the light of men." Jesus Christ revealed the truth.

   e) John 8:12—Jesus said, "I am the light of the world; he that followeth me shall not walk in darkness, but shall have the light of life." In the verses following, Jesus talked about truth.

   Here are more Scriptures that talk about the same thing: John 12:35-36, 46; Acts 13:46-47; 26:18, 23; 2 Corinthians 4:4-6; 2 Peter 1:9. Intellectually, light speaks of knowledge of the truth. Darkness speaks of ignorance or error.

2. The moral aspect

   Morally, light refers to holiness, and darkness refers to impurity.

26

a) Romans 13:11-12—"Knowing the time, that now it is high time to awake out of sleep; for now is our salvation nearer than when we believed. The night is far spent, the day is at hand; let us, therefore, cast off the works of darkness, and let us put on the armor of light." "The works of darkness" have to do with moral evil, and "the armor of light" has to do with moral goodness—not reveling in drunkenness and immoral behavior (v. 13).

b) 1 Thessalonians 5:4-5, 7—"Ye, brethren, are not in darkness, that that day [the day of the Lord's return] should overtake you as a thief. Ye are all sons of light, and sons of the day; we are not of the night, nor of darkness. . . . For they that sleep sleep in the night; and they that are drunk are drunk in the night."

B. Applying the Definitions of Light and Darkness

1. To God

The apostle John said, "God is light" (1 John 1:5). According to the definitions established by Scripture, the intellectual aspect of light leads us to see that God is truth, and the moral aspect teaches that He is holy. John said at the end of verse 5, "In him is no darkness at all." There is no error or evil in God. In the Greek text John's statement is written as a double negative, which is the strongest negative possible. He was saying, "God is absolutely perfect; He is without blemish or sin. There is nothing in His character to impinge upon the absolute character of light." James 1:17 says, "Every good gift and every perfect gift is from above, and cometh down from the Father of lights, with whom is no variableness, neither shadow of turning." God cannot vary from truth and holiness.

First John 1:5 describes the essential character of God. It describes the essential distinction between the true and the false, the good and the evil, the holy and the sinful, and the innocent and the guilty. The Greek text of 1 John 1:5 literally says there is not a single bit of darkness in God. That is the basic truth of the passage and is the foundation for what we are about to learn from the verses that follow.

2. To people

Those who are in the fellowship are one with God. First

27

Corinthians 6:17 says, "He that is joined unto the Lord is one spirit." All Christians are one with God. Since that is true, are Christians in the light or in darkness? They are in the light because God is light. Is it possible for a Christian to be in darkness? No, there is no darkness in the light. First John 1:6 says, "If we say that we have fellowship with him [God], and walk in darkness, we lie, and do not the truth." Many people have said that passage refers to a Christian who is in the light but beginning to walk into darkness. However, there is no darkness in God; that is clear from Scripture. Believers are in the light; they cannot walk in darkness. That is the basis of John's argument distinguishing the true believer from the false. God is light and in Him is no darkness at all; therefore if we are in Him, we are in the light.

You say, "How can I be in the light and still be a sinner?" That is possible because when you sin you are instantly cleansed. Practically speaking, there are sins in our lives that we need to deal with. But in God's sight, the blood of Christ continually cleanses us so that no darkness ever enters the light. You can almost say we are cleansed in anticipation that we will sin. If sin ever did emerge in the light, there would be darkness in it, and that can't be. Let's look now at the contrast between those who claim to be in the light and those who really are in the light.

II. THE DISTINCTION (vv. 1:6—2:1a)

In the verses immediately following 1 John 1:5, the apostle talks about two groups of people: those who merely claim to be in the fellowship and those who really are in it.

A. Those Who Say They Are Christians (vv. 6, 8, 10)

1. The clarification

   John uses the word *we* in verses 6, 8, and 10. Many people think he is referring to Christians in those verses. However, "we" doesn't have to refer to Christians. I could say, "We in our country must turn to God." Does that mean I haven't already turned to God? No. *We* can be used in a general way. John uses the first person plural in verses 6, 8, and 10 because he is stating a general principle that is applicable to all men.

28

The Sin Test

Some of the gnostics John confronted said, "I am in the light." There are many people today who say, "I'm a Christian; I believe in God." To find out if that is true, just ask a person to explain his view of sin. That's a good test to use to find out if someone is really in the light. In 1 John 1, there are three erroneous claims (in verses 6, 8, and 10) that John puts to the test. They have to do with our conduct, our nature, and our relation to God. In each case, John focuses on the reality of sin. He shows that the way to God involves confessing sin, accepting God's provision for cleansing, and never denying the reality of sin.

2. The claims

   a) Expressed

   Verse six begins, "If we say that we have fellowship with him." Would you say there are many people who claim that? There are liberal churches and false religions filled with people who claim to have fellowship with God. If we say we have fellowship with God, yet "walk in darkness, we lie, and do not the truth" (v. 6). If someone claims to be a Christian but walks in darkness, he is a liar. A person in the fellowship—someone who is in the light—cannot be in darkness. In verse 8 John says, "If we say that we have no sin, we deceive ourselves, and the truth is not in us." Then he says in verse 10, "If we say that we have not sinned, we make him a liar, and his word is not in us." So John described the claimers. They said, "We are in the fellowship," but he said, "Really? You say you are in the fellowship, but you walk in darkness. You claim to have no sin, but you are self-deceived. You say you have never sinned and make God a liar." What is the attitude of the claimers toward sin in all three verses? They deny it. I said earlier that it's a very basic thing to admit sin. If a man never admits he is a sinner, he will never have the proper perspective toward God that can result in salvation. Rather than agreeing with God, saying the same thing that God says about his sin, he denies it.

   The man described in verse 6 doesn't confess his sin because he doesn't think that's necessary. He is satisfied to walk in darkness and claim to be in the fellowship. He says to himself, "I may be doing some

29

bad things, but I'm in the fellowship. Even though I sin a lot, I remember when I received the Lord. I know what Christianity is all about; I'm OK." It's fine to say that if you are really in the fellowship, but if you walk in darkness and say those things, you are a liar. The man in verse 8 doesn't confess his sin because he claims to have reached the state where no sin exists. His sin nature no longer bothers him. He says, "My sin nature is removed; I'm perfectly all right." The gnostics said there was no sin in their real selves. The man in verse 10 doesn't confess his sin because he claims, "I have never sinned at all in my whole life!" Can you imagine anyone's saying that? I have met people who say they don't see themselves as sinners.

b) Examined

The problem with the people described in verses 6, 8, and 10 is that they fail John's test regarding the right perspective on sin. There are three words that describe such people.

(1) Darkness (v. 6)

"If we say that we have fellowship with him, and walk in darkness, we lie, and do not the truth."

(a) The refutation of the claim

These people claim to be in the fellowship, yet they really aren't. They have invaded the church, saying, "We are Christians. We believe what the Bible says. You know we talk about Christ. We share in the common eternal life with God and are partners in His nature." John says, "Let's look at your walk—your manner of life—because you can tell what a man is by what he does. If you say you are in the fellowship but your manner of life continues to remain in darkness, you are a liar." John said it isn't what one claims that matters but how one acts. The person who is in the fellowship is in the light and will display the characteristics of God. If you are in the fellowship, your life will be characterized by holiness. But if you say you are a partaker of the divine nature (2 Pet. 1:4) yet habitually participate in the deeds of darkness, you are a liar.

Paul said, "If any man be in Christ, he is a new creation; old things are passed away; behold, all things are become new" (2 Cor. 5:17). A person who is in the fellowship is in the light and must have the characteristics of the light. The word "walk" in 1 John 1:6 is in the linear present tense: it refers to someone who is habitually in darkness. If a person lives like that, he cannot be a Christian. Any claim to the contrary is a lie. A person who lives a life of sin is not in the fellowship because he is not in the light. Some of the gnostics who claimed to be in the light were blatant sinners. They were absolutely amoral, yet claimed that had no effect on their spirits. There are some people today who claim to have a mystical intimacy with God apart from a holy life, and, like the gnostics, they are liars.

(b) The requirement for obedience

True religion without morality is nonexistent. In 2 Corinthians 6:14 Paul asks, "What communion hath light with darkness?" None! There can't be a communion of light and darkness. So if you claim to be in the light yet walk in darkness, you "lie, and do not the truth" (1 John 1:6). The present tense is used in that phrase, making it literally read, "You are habitually not doing the truth."

Notice that John said those who walk in darkness "*do* not the truth." Truth is not simply something to be believed; it is to be acted upon. Salvation is not simply a matter of believing in Christ; it is a matter of living in obedience to Him. If you say you are in the fellowship but the manner of your life is continuously sinful, you are a liar. Truth is to be practiced. James said if your faith is genuine, your works will reveal it (2:17). He also said, "Be ye doers of the word and not hearers only, deceiving your own selves" (1:22). First John 3:2-3 says, "Beloved, now

31

are we the children of God, and it doth not yet appear what we shall be, but we know that, when he shall appear, we shall be like him; for we shall see him as he is. And every man that hath this hope in him purifieth himself even as he is pure." Holiness goes with salvation.

In 3 John 11 we read, "Beloved, follow not that which is evil, but that which is good. He that doeth good is of God, but he that doeth evil hath not seen God." Again, John states the test for distinguishing a true believer from a false one. There is no such thing as true religion without morality. You aren't saved by your good works, but salvation results in good works (Eph. 2:8-10). So, the truth is not just a creed. It is a kind of life. When someone says, "I'm in the fellowship; I'm in the light," but is characterized by darkness, he is a liar.

Can a Christian ever be in darkness?

1. The opinion

Some people say 1 John 1:6 talks about people who are saved but have begun to walk in sin. Only God knows where each person really stands in regard to the sin in his life, but John is saying that you can't be a Christian and habitually walk in sin. He writes in chapter 3, "Ye know that he [Christ] was manifested to take away our sins, and in him is no sin. Whosoever abideth in him sinneth not; whosoever sinneth hath not seen him, neither known him. . . . Whosoever is born of God doth not commit sin; for his seed remaineth in him, and he cannot sin, because he is born of God" (vv. 5-6, 9). Holiness accompanies true salvation.

At this point, someone still might insist that 1 John 1:6 talks about Christians who are walking in darkness. But how can a Christian walk in darkness if he is one with God, in whom there is no darkness at all? How can a person say John is talking about a Christian there? Someone might say, "By inference."

2. The facts

Let's look at some direct references and see what they say.

a) Acts 26:18—Jesus wanted Paul to preach to the Gentiles "to open their eyes, and to turn them from darkness to light." That verse is talking about salvation—turning people from darkness to light. Salvation is light, not darkness.

b) John 8:12—The Lord said, "I am the light of the world; he that followeth me shall not walk in darkness." Can a Christian walk in darkness? Christ said no!

c) Ephesians 5:1-2, 8—"Be ye, therefore, followers of God, as dear children; and walk in love. . . . For ye were once darkness, but now are ye light in the Lord; walk as children of light." We are to walk as children of light (v. 13).

d) Colossians 1:12-13—"[God] hath made us fit to be partakers of the inheritance of the saints in light" (v. 12). We have been translated into the kingdom of light.

e) 1 Thessalonians 5:4-5—"Ye, brethren, are not in darkness. . . . Ye are all sons of light, and sons of the day; we are not of the night, nor of darkness."

f) 1 Peter 2:9—"Ye are a chosen generation, a royal priesthood, an holy nation, a people of his own, that ye should show forth the praises of him who hath called you out of darkness into his marvelous light."

Can a Christian walk in darkness? No. Saying someone is in the light is like saying he is saved. If you are going to say a Christian can be in darkness, you will have to say that a person can be saved and unsaved at the same time. A believer cannot walk in darkness because he is one with God, Christ, and the Spirit. God is light, and in Him is no darkness. You say, "What happens if I sin?" When you sin, you do so in the light. God will reveal your sin and cleanse you of it. We will all sin once in a while—but not habitually. First John 2:12 has some reassuring words for us: "I write unto you, little children, because your sins are forgiven you for his name's sake." "Your sins are forgiven" is in the past

33

tense—your sins have all been taken care of by the cross. Some people say the cross only took care of the sins you committed up to the time you became saved and that you have to take care of the sins that happen from that point on. Don't believe that. Christ bore all our sins in His body (Heb. 10:10, 14). Positionally, we are cleansed. Darkness cannot enter into our fellowship with God; it cannot intrude into the light of God. We may occasionally stumble and do deeds of darkness, but if we do, we do so in full light.

Some of those who claim to be in the fellowship are in darkness. Others of them are characterized by:

(2) Deceit (v.8)

"If we say that we have no sin, we deceive ourselves, and the truth is not in us."

(a) Denying the reality of sin

This claim is worse than the first. The person in verse 6 says, "It doesn't matter if I sin. I'm in the fellowship and the light, and although I make many mistakes, I'm all right." But the person here says, "I have no sin. My sin nature has been set aside." The first person concedes the existence of sin, but this person denies he even sins anymore. Some gnostics used to say, "Sin is only in my flesh. My true self—my spirit—is absolutely sinless." The person who says that nullifies the cleansing blood of Christ, because in his mind there's nothing to cleanse.

The word "sin" in verse 8 is singular, which indicates that John is referring to the inherited principle of sin. The claim literally reads, "I don't sin anymore." Anyone who says that deceives himself. You can't attribute sin to a psychological disease or say that it comes from stress. That is willful blindness and self-deceit; don't kid yourself. John says at the end of verse 8 that if we do that, "The truth is not in us." The person in verse 6 simply doesn't obey the truth; the person in verse 8 doesn't even possess it. At least the

34

person in verse 6 admits sin exists, even though he doesn't think it matters. The person in verse 8 doesn't even admit sin exists in him; therefore, he doesn't have the truth. To claim sinlessness is to be void of truth.

(b) Declaring the reality of sin

The Scripture is clear about sin. Earlier, I listed some verses in which people confessed their sin. There are more verses that talk about sin.

i) Ecclesiastes 7:20 — "There is not a just man upon earth, that doeth good and sinneth not."

ii) Romans 3:23 — "For all have sinned, and come short of the glory of God."

iii) Romans 3:12—Paul said, "There is none that doeth good." In case anyone might say, "I'm an exception," Paul ended that statement with these words: "No, not one."

iv) 2 Chronicles 6:36—"There is no man who sinneth not." That includes those who think they have reached a state of perfection from a second work of grace from God.

There is no man without sin. No man can deny sin and claim to have a relationship with God. A person might say, "I'm in the fellowship and the light," but if he denies sin, he is deceiving himself. Sin is real. To deny it is self-deceit. A man who denies his sin lives in darkness, and the result is tragic. He not only is unaware of his darkness but is also convinced he's OK when he's not. Proverbs 28:13 says, "He that covereth his sins shall not prosper."

In 1 John 1:10 there appears a third claim from someone who says he is a Christian but really isn't. This person doesn't just lie about being in the fellowship and say that he has no sin nature. In addition to those things, he lies about his actions and makes God a liar. That person is characterized by the word:

(3) Defamation (v.10)

"If we say that we have not sinned, we make him [God] a liar, and his word is not in us."

That is the ultimate claim. The person in verse 6 admits sin is in his life. The person in verse 8 says he used to sin but is now perfect. However, this person says he has never sinned! Such a person makes God a liar, and God's Word is not in him. The gnostics used to say their superior knowledge made them incapable of sinning. It's one thing to lie, but it's worse to deceive yourself, because not only are you trapped into being oblivious to your sin, but you are also slandering God. Someone who does that is definitely not in the fellowship.

Paul said in Titus 1:2 that "God . . . cannot lie." Jesus said to the Father, "Thy word is truth" (John 17:17). God has no capacity to lie whatsoever. First John 5:10 says, "He that believeth on the Son of God hath the witness in himself; he that believeth not God hath made him a liar, because he believeth not the record that God gave of his Son." If you don't agree with God about Christ, you are a liar. The same is true about you if you don't agree with God about sin. People who deny Jesus Christ not only lie themselves, but also make God a liar.

Denying sin results in darkness, deceit, and defamation. Those who deny their sin do not walk in the light, no matter what they may claim. They are not partakers of eternal life; they are false Christians. They say they are Christians but don't live like it. First John 1:7 and 9 present a contrast: "If we walk in the light. . . . If we confess our sins." True believers walk in the light and confess their sins. They don't just make claims. False Christians fail the test on the doctrine of sin. They don't say the same thing about sin that God says.

I do not say these things out of anger, malice, or bitterness; I say them with a sense of urgency. I share the truth because I know the tragedy that awaits those who reject the truth. A man must see that he has violated the law of God. The greatest of all sins is failing to love the Lord your God with all your heart, soul, mind, and strength (Deut. 6:5; Matt. 22:37). The second greatest sin is to fail to love your neighbor as yourself (Matt. 22:39). The supreme sin is to reject Jesus Christ as Savior and Lord. All men are guilty of sin (Rom. 3:23). It is foolish to deny that and, as a result, deceive yourself and slander God.

You say, "What do I do if I recognize that I'm a sinner?" The first thing you need to do is come to Jesus Christ, who is in the business of forgiving sin and cleansing people. He wants to help you, but He can't until you recognize that you are a sinner.

Focusing on the Facts

1. What is one of the more important truths recorded in the Bible? Give some examples (see p. 20).

2. Acknowledgment of sin is basic to what (Josh. 7:19; see p. 22)?

3. What does Romans 1:32 say? What is the only way man can eliminate the fear he gets from knowing that (see p. 22)?

4. With what do some people associate the refusal to face sin? Is that necessarily true? Explain (see p. 22).

5. In what ways did the Israelites offend God, according to the book of Malachi (see pp. 22-23)?

6. What are some of the things Satan says when he propagates false doctrine about sin (see p. 24)?

7. What did the gnostics teach about sin (see pp. 24-25)?

8. The message John was preaching was not _____ ; it was a _____ from _____ (1 John 1:5; see p. 26).

9. What do light and darkness speak of from an intellectual aspect? What do they refer to from a moral aspect (see pp. 26-27)?

10. Discuss what John was communicating when he said, "In [God] is no darkness at all" (1 John 1:5; see p. 27).

11. How do we know all Christians are in the light (Cor. 6:17; see pp. 27-28)?

12. Discuss what happens when a believer sins in the light (see p. 28).

13. What is a good test to use when determining if someone is really in the light (see p. 29)?

14. Explain why the people in verses 6, 9, and 10 don't confess their sins (see pp. 29-30).

15. How did John refute the claim made in verse 6? What will your life be characterized by if you are in the fellowship (see pp. 30-31)?

16. John said those who walk in darkness "*do* not the truth" (1 John 1:6). What is the significance of that statement? Use Scripture to support your answer (see pp. 31-32).

17. What do some people think 1 John 1:6 talks about? Does the Bible support that? Explain, supporting your answer with Scripture (see pp. 32-33).

18. What does 1 John 2:12 tell us in regard to our sins? Why is that important (see pp. 33-34)?

19. What claim does the person in 1 John 1:8 make? What does a person who says that nullify? Why (see pp. 34-35)?

20. Is any man without sin? What does the Bible say (see pp. 34-35)?

21. What does a person who says he has never sinned essentially say about God (1 John 1:10; see pp. 35-36)?

22. What is the greatest of all sins? What must a person do when he recognizes he is a sinner (see p. 37)?

Pondering the Principles

1. Read the following verses, and write down what you learn about sin: Habakkuk 1:13; Romans 5:12; 1 John 3:4, 8-10. What effect does sin have on man's ability to discern spiritual things (1 Cor. 2:14)? What are some of the results of sin (Gen. 6:5; Eph. 2:1; 4:18; James 4:1)? Based on what you have learned, define sin and explain the perspective Christians should have toward it.

2. A Christian, because he is one with God, lives in the light. However, there are times when a believer is tempted to sin. Jesus is the perfect role model of how to properly respond to temptation. According to Matthew 4:1-11, how did Jesus respond to temptation from the devil? What did He do in Matthew 26:36-44 before He was faced with particularly difficult circumstances? What did Christ say to His disciples in verse 41? Be committed to saturating your mind with God's Word and praying regularly so you can be prepared to respond to temptation in the right way.

3. Reread the material on pages 29-32. Determine what you would say to someone who believes it is possible for a Christian to walk in darkness.

3
If We Confess Our Sins—
Part 2

Outline

Introduction
A. The Concealment of Sin
B. The Condemnation of Sin
C. The Confession of Sin

Review
I. The Declaration
II. The Distinction
   A. Those Who Say They Are Christians
      1. The clarification
      2. The claims
         a) Expressed
         b) Examined
            (1) Darkness
            (2) Deceit
            (3) Defamation

Lesson
B. Those Who Really Are Christians
     1. Cleansed
        a) The character
        b) The companionship
           (1) The Person of the companionship
           (2) The nature of the companionship
        c) The cleansing
           (1) The fact stated
           (2) The fact supported
              (*a*) Ephesians 1:7
              (*b*) Hebrews 9:14
              (*c*) Hebrews 10:14
     2. Confession

        a) The prerequisite
        b) The promise
        c) The perspectives
           (1) The Socinian view
           (2) The psychological view
           (3) The salvationist view
           (4) The conditional view
           (5) The correct view
        d) The particulars
           (1) Sorrow over sin
           (2) Repentance
    3. Conquering
        a) The complacency
        b) The command
III. The Deliverance
    A. Christ the advocate
    B. Christ the appeaser
        1. For all believers
        2. For all the world

Conclusion

When The Covered They Nakidnsse They wem Admitting Their o

Introduction

    A. The Concealment of Sin

We have all fought many times the battle of whether to admit a wrongdoing or to cover it up. You can go back to the book of Genesis and find that the first man alive, Adam, was caught in that dilemma. He sinned and had two options: He could either confess his sin to God, or he could hide it. What did he do? He hid from God. He and his wife made aprons from fig leaves to cover themselves up physically. Every man has faced the dilemma of whether to confess sin or cover it up. Proverbs 28:13 says, "He that covereth his sins shall not prosper, but whoso confesseth and forsaketh them shall have mercy." God says it is much better to confess your sin than to hide it.

The practice of concealing sin is characteristic of unbelievers. They do not acknowledge their sin; therefore, they will not prosper, according to Proverbs 28:13. They are on the broad road that leads to destruction (Matt. 7:13). But Christians confess their sin, prosper from God's mercy, and are on the narrow road that leads to glory (Matt. 7:14). One of the distinctions between an unbeliever and a believer is the confession of sin.

B. The Condemnation of Sin

There is coming a day when there will be no secrets. First Corinthians 4 clearly indicates that the Lord "will bring to light the hidden things of darkness, and will make manifest the counsels of the hearts" (v. 5). That passage refers to believers, but the general truth is that someday everyone's heart will be disclosed. For the godly, that will bring reward, but for the ungodly, that will bring damnation. God will reveal and judge all sin that has been covered up, but the sin that had been exposed and cleansed by the blood of Christ will never be exposed again. When we who are believers go to heaven, God will not show us our sins because they have already been taken care of.

God is stern in judging sin because ultimately it is always against Him. All sin is against God. The story about David and Bathsheba exemplifies that. David saw Bathsheba from the palace roof when she was bathing on her roof. He was attracted by her beauty. He lusted after her, took her for himself, and she became pregnant. Then David arranged the murder of her husband. He broke four of the last five commandments; he coveted, he stole, he committed adultery, and he murdered someone. When he repented, this is what he said: "Against thee, thee only, have I sinned, and done this evil in thy sight" (Ps. 51:4). David wasn't denying that he sinned against himself (any kind of adultery is sin against your own body [1 Cor. 6:18]). He didn't deny that he had sinned against Bathsheba, her husband, Uriah, and the whole nation of Israel. David recognized that sin is primarily against God. So true confession is not just admitting you sinned; it involves admitting you sinned against God. True confession recognizes that sin is an affront to God.

C. The Confession of Sin

In 1 John 1:5 — 2:2, the apostle John talks about the confession of sin as a test of salvation. A person's view of sin is an indicator of whether he is saved, no matter what he claims. Among those to whom John wrote his first epistle were the gnostics. They claimed to be Christians. John said, "If you want to know if someone truly is a Christian, don't just listen to his claims. Test his views." First the apostle asked, "What is the person's view of Christ?" (1 John 1:1-4). Some gnostics taught that Jesus was a phantom, not the Christ that was revealed in the New Testament. Other gnostics said that a Christ spirit merely descended on the man Jesus and then left

43

again. They had a wrong view of Christ. Later on, John talked about the test of obedience—the issue of whether people obeyed the law of God. He also talked about the test of love for the brethren. If someone who professes to be a Christian loves those who are in Christ, that's evidence of spiritual life; if he doesn't, he shows he is not what he claims to be. The test John talks about in 1 John 1:6—2:1 looks at a person's view of sin, focusing on whether he confesses sin.

The word *confess* (Gk., *homologeō*) means "to say the same thing." Do those who claim to be Christians say the same thing about sin that God says about it? Likewise, do they confess that Jesus is the Son of God (1 John 4:15)? Do they say the same thing about Christ that God says about Him? It's easy for people to claim they are Christians and say they are in the fellowship and light. But do they say the same thing about sin that God does? If not, they are false teachers, deceivers, and antichrists. The test of one's view of sin is very simple.

Review

Let's look at the premise on which 1 John 1:6—2:1 is built.

I. THE DECLARATION (1.5)

"This, then, is the message which we have heard of him, and declare unto you, that God is light, and in him is no darkness at all." *Even the physical Sun has Sun Spots dark patches—*
God is absolute light. Intellectually, light refers to truth; morally, it refers to holiness. God is absolute truth and holiness. No error or defilement exists in Him. Therefore, if someone claims to be in Him, he will be without error and undefiled. He will have the truth and will live a holy life. A Christian is always holy positionally; there is no exception. Only cleansed people belong to God because He is light, and there is no darkness in Him. Anyone who is not cleansed from sin—no matter what he says to the contrary—is not in the light, because the light has no darkness in it. The only people who are in the light are those who have been cleansed from their sins by Jesus Christ. That is John's basic premise.

II. THE DISTINCTION (1:6—2:1*a*)

In 1 John 1:6—2:1, the apostle divides his message into two parts. First, he talks about those who claim to be in the fellowship (1:6,

8, 10), then he talks about those who are in the fellowship (1:7; 9; 2:1).

A. Those Who Say They Are Christians (1:6, 8, 10)

Among those to whom John wrote were people who were saying they were Christians when that wasn't true. To help expose them, John said, "Let's check out their doctrine of sin."

1. The clarification

2. The claims

   a) Expressed

   b) Examined

      (1) Darkness (1:6)

      "If we say that we have fellowship with him, and walk in darkness, we lie, and do not the truth."

      A person cannot have fellowship with God and walk in darkness because "in him is no darkness at all" (1 John 1:5). Someone who perpetually walks in sin can never be identified with the fellowship of God. Such a person says, "I sin a lot, but that's all right. I'm still in the light. Sin has no effect on me. It's only my flesh that sins; my spirit is OK." That person is characterized by darkness. If you're perpetually involved in sin, you can't claim to be in the light. You are a liar, and you "do not the truth."

      (2) Deceit (1:8)

      "If we say that we have no sin, we deceive ourselves, and the truth is not in us."

      Some of the gnostics John was confronting actually said they had reached a point in their lives where they no longer sinned. A person who denies that sin exists in him is void of the truth, because sin exists in everyone. Denying sin doesn't make it go away.

      (3) Defamation (1:10)

      "If we say that we have not sinned, we make him a liar, and his word is not in us.

45

Of course you don't actually make God a liar but your wound the weaker + the lost who may have confidence in you.

John has described in three verses people who deny sin. Verse 6 talks about those characterized by darkness, verse 8 talks about those characterized by deceit, and verse 10 talks about those who defame God. They slander Him and make Him a liar by saying, "We have not sinned," when the Bible says that everyone has sinned. Romans 3:23 says "all have sinned, and come short of the glory of God." Romans 3:10-19 talks about the same thing. No matter what a person claims, if he walks in darkness, self-deceit, and slanders the character of God, he is not a Christian. It all boils down to the test of denying sin: If someone covers up his sin, he is not a Christian. That's not the only test of genuine salvation, but it's a very important one. Sin is not a popular thing to admit today.

Let's look now at the group of people who are in the fellowship. We will be looking at what a Christian is.

Lesson

B. Those Who Really Are Christians (1:7, 9; 2:1a)

We will use three words to describe believers, just as we used three words to describe unbelievers.

1. Cleansed (1:7) *– 2 – Confession – 3 – Conquering*

"But if we walk in the light, as He is in the light, we have fellowship one with another, and the blood of Jesus Christ, his Son, cleanseth us from all sin."

a) The character (1:7*a*)

"But if we walk in the light, as he is in the light."

The word translated "walk" is a present tense subjunctive that refers to continuous action. It's an indicator of character. John was saying, "If we are habitually in the light, as God is in the light, we have fellowship with Him."

Who is in the light? Christians. They share in God's life and light, for there is no darkness in God. If you are a Christian, you are in the light. That is the definition of a Christian.

46

b) The companionship (1:7*b*)

"We have fellowship one with another."

How do you know who is in the fellowship? Those who are in the light are. How do you know if you are in the light? You are if you have come to know God.

(1) The Person of the companionship

The word "another" in 1 John 1:7 does not refer to other Christians but to God. We can know that by looking at more of the verse: "But if we walk in the light, as he is in the light, we have fellowship one with another, and the blood of Jesus Christ, his Son . . ." The word "his" modifies "another," so the word "another" refers to God.

(2) The nature of the companionship

If we walk in the light, we have fellowship with God. The nature of our fellowship with Him is reciprocal: it's "one with another." Our fellowship goes back and forth. We share a common life with God. Keep in mind that it is not something we experience at this time; John is talking about the believer's positional union with God.

Those who walk in the light are in the fellowship. That simply means that those who are saved are in the light and fellowship. To say someone who's walking habitually in darkness is in the fellowship is wrong. There is no darkness in God. But if we have received Jesus Christ, we have entered into the light, for He is the light. Believers walk in the light and share the common life of God. The word "fellowship" in the Greek text of 1 John 1:7 means "partaker." We are partakers with God; we have partnership "one with another."

c) The cleansing (1:7*c*)

"And the blood of Jesus Christ, his Son, cleanseth us from all sin."

(1) The fact stated

The blood of Christ didn't just cleanse us of some sins; it cleansed us of *all* sins. The blood Christ shed on the cross is a symbol of His death. Peter used that symbol when he said we "were not redeemed with corruptible things, like silver and

47

gold, from your vain manner of life . . . but with the precious blood of Christ, as of a lamb without blemish and without spot" (1 Pet. 1:18-19). Christ's blood is the symbol of His death, which was completely efficacious for us. His blood was shed on our behalf at one time, and it is a constant provision for our cleansing. Revelation 1:5-6 says, "Jesus Christ, who is the faithful witness, and the first begotten of the dead, and the prince of the kings of the earth. Unto him that loveth us, and washed us from our sins in his own blood . . . be glory and dominion forever." The blood Christ shed paid the price for our sins and became a cleansing agent that washed them away. The blood itself didn't have some special quality; it was Christ's giving of His life that paid the penalty for sin, and that is symbolized by the shedding of His blood.

First John 1:7 says Christ's blood *"cleanseth* us from all sin" (emphasis added). There is only one condition for cleansing: you must be walking in the light. If you do that, you are a Christian; and if you are a believer, you have absolute and continuous cleansing of all sin. That's what verse 7 is saying. Confession of sin is not a condition for cleansing. Salvation is the only condition. If you are in the light, you are one with God.

(2) The fact supported

    (*a*) Ephesians 1:7

        When a person becomes a Christian, he receives "redemption through [Christ's] blood [and] the forgiveness of sins, according to the riches of His grace." Our forgiveness is in accordance with the riches of the Lord's grace. And how rich is He? Rich enough to cover all our sins.

    (*b*) Hebrews 9:14

        We read here, "How much more shall the blood of Christ, who through the eternal Spirit offered himself without spot to God, purge your conscience from dead works?" The blood of Jesus Christ totally purges us.

(c) Hebrews 10:14

The writer of Hebrews wrote, "For by one offering [Christ] hath perfected forever them that are sanctified." Christ's one offering brought us total cleansing. Not just for now, but for all eternity.

It's fantastic to realize that we are always in the light when we are in God because He is in the light. Even when we sin, we are still in the light because God deals with that sin instantly, cleansing us as a result of the perfect and total efficacy of Christ.

You Need Only One Bath

John 13 has an illustration of how Christ's sacrifice cleanses us forever. Jesus gave some insight into the matter when He washed the disciples' feet. In verse 10, Christ says to Peter, "He that is washed needeth not except to wash his feet, but is entirely clean; and ye are clean, but not all of you." (That last statement refers to Judas.) Jesus was saying this: "Once you have been cleansed, all your sins have been forgiven. Only the dust of the world needs to be washed off your feet, and I will continually take care of that." That's a beautiful promise. If you are already saved, you don't need to be cleansed again—you don't need to take another bath. John 13:10 is a picture of the positional cleansing and holiness of the believer at salvation. Christ will continue to keep us clean every day as we walk through the world. How many baths do you need? One. A person needs to be saved only once.

John 13:10 shows that salvation is a one-time event. You don't need to get saved again and again. John 15:3 says, "Ye are clean through the word." That is salvation; once is all it takes.

So, the believer is described by the word *cleansed*. Next, he is described by the word

2. Confession (1:9)

"If we confess our sins, he is faithful and just to forgive us our sins, and to cleanse us from all unrighteousness."

a) The prerequisite

You say, "Wait a minute. You just said there isn't any condition for cleansing." That's right. There is no condition for cleansing in verse 7. The only reason there appears to be one in verse 9 is that verse 7 looks at salvation from God's perspective and verse 9 looks at it from ours.

You say, "Verse 7 tells us God takes care of our sins automatically, but now verse 9 says we must confess our sins. So there is a condition for forgiveness." No, there isn't. God instantly forgives and cleanses people because of Christ's death, but He only does that to those who are confessing their sins. In effect, 1 John 1:9 reads, "If we are the ones confessing our sins, He is forgiving us." God only forgives those who are confessing their sins—that is, Christians. Who are the people who aren't confessing their sins? Non-Christians. John wasn't saying, "You must confess your sins or God won't forgive you." Rather, he was saying, "God is constantly cleansing the sins of those who are confessing."

One definition of a Christian is this: He is someone who agrees with God that he is a sinner. You aren't a Christian if you haven't done that. No one can enter into God's kingdom without admitting he is a sinner and that he needs Christ. So those who admit they are sinners are the ones God cleanses. Some people say, "What about someone who once confessed his sins but doesn't do that anymore?" Such a person probably wasn't ever cleansed to begin with. One sign of true salvation is that a person will continue to confess his sin.

b) The promise

Notice that John said, "[God] is faithful and just to forgive." God promised He would be merciful to those who confessed their sins (Prov. 28:13). In Jeremiah 31, the Lord says, "I will forgive their iniquity, and I will remember their sin no more" (v. 34). God promised to forgive, and He is faithful to do so.

You say, "What did John mean when he said that God is 'just to forgive'? How could God be just and forgive sin? That would be like a judge telling someone who murdered eight people, 'You can go. I forgive you.' That's not justice!" But this is how God can be just and forgive sin: Jesus Christ paid the penalty for our sins, so justice is satisfied. Romans 3 says Jesus was crucified to display the justice of God so that we might know He is just and the justifier of those who believe in Christ (vv. 25-26). The same truth is reflected in verses 7 and 9 of 1 John 1. Verse 7 says He forgives because of what Christ did, and verse 9 emphasizes that His forgiveness is extended to those who admit they are sinners.

One interesting thing I want to point out is that the tenses and grammar in the Greek text of the New Testament add meaning to a passage. The word translated "forgive" in 1 John 1:9 is in the aorist tense, which means John was not talking about continuous forgiveness but a single act of forgiveness. First John 1:9 talks about God's forgiving individual acts of sin, not habitual sin. Christians don't sin habitually, but they do sin infrequently. First John 3:9 says, "Whosoever is born of God doth not commit sin." Someone who continually lives in sin is not of God. But God takes care of us each time we sin.

c) The perspectives

There are many views of confession. Let's look at some of them.

(1) The Socinian view

Faustus Socinius, a sixteenth-century religious leader, said that the word "confess" in 1 John 1:9 doesn't literally refer to confessing your sins; it just means we are to be conscious of them. Socinius wanted to get away from the idea of agreeing with what God said about sin. But that violates the meaning of the word translated "confess" (Gk., *homologeō*), which means saying the same thing God does about your sins. First John 1:9 doesn't say you are merely to be conscious of them.

(2) The psychological view

One adhering to this view says, "You don't really have to confess your sins because God is taking care of them. You only need to confess them so that you are involved with what's going on, which is good therapy. Confessing your sins teaches you humility and pain. God wants to refine you through your sorrow; you need to pour your heart out." However, that interpretation doesn't explain what 1 John 1:9 says.

(3) The salvationist view

There are some people who teach that the forgiveness in 1 John 1:9 applies only to the time you get saved. That's a very popular teaching now. But that does terrible injustice to the word translated "confess," which is in the present tense and refers to habitual confession. Confessing sin isn't just a one-time thing.

(4) The conditional view

The most popular view of all is that forgiveness is conditional on confession: When a Christian sins, fellowship with God is broken and can only be restored when the sin is confessed. Many of us have heard this formula: Sin breaks fellowship, and confession restores it. However, fellowship can't be broken, so that theory is out.

Commentator Roy Laurin said, "Confessed sin will be forgiven. . . . Unconfessed sins will remain in a person until the Judgment Seat of Christ; then He will deal with them. . . . Sin can never be cleansed from us until it is forgiven in us, and it is never forgiven in us until it has been confessed by us" (*Life at Its Best: Studies in the First Epistle of John* [Los Angeles: Church of the Open Door, 1939], pp. 24-25). He was saying that a Christian can have unforgiven sins.

(5) The correct view

First John 2:12 says, "I write unto you, little children, because your sins are forgiven." A believer can't have unforgiven sins. You say, "That's only one verse." Read Colossians 2:13: "And you, being dead in your sins and the uncircumcision of your flesh, hath he made alive together with him, *having forgiven* you all trespasses" (emphasis added). The phrase "having forgiven" is past tense. Ephesians 4:32 says, "Be ye kind one to another, tenderhearted, forgiving one another, even as God, for Christ's sake, hath forgiven you." Paul said, "You are to forgive as God forgave." That's all in the past tense. Christ

52

told Peter to forgive "seventy times seven" (Matt. 18:22). God has forgiven us at least that many times!

First John 1:9 does not say if we confess one sin, we are forgiven once; if we confess two sins, we are forgiven twice; and if we forget one sin, God zaps us. John was saying, "God is forgiving those who are agreeing they are sinners." The flow of forgiveness is toward the person who continuously acknowledges to God that he is a sinner. Such a person shows evidence of being forgiven; he shows he is a true Christian.

The gnostics used to say, "The Lord has taken care of my sins. They are all gone." But John said, "If you aren't confessing your sins and agreeing with what God says about sin, then you aren't among those being forgiven." One mark of a Christian is that he continuously confesses his sinfulness.

Continual Confession Characterizes Christians

This concept can be illustrated by the word *faith*. How does a person become saved? By grace through faith (Eph. 2:8-9). After a person is saved, does faith stop? No. Some people say, "I'm saved now; I can quit believing." That's not right. If your faith is real it will continue. Belief is not a one-time thing; it is constant.

1. 1 John 5:1—"Whosoever believeth that Jesus is the Christ is born of God." In the King James Version, the word "believeth" sounds like a one-time action. However, in the Greek text, that word is in the present tense, making the verse literally read, "Whosoever continues to believe."

2. John 8:31—"If ye continue in my word, then are ye my disciples indeed."

3. 1 John 2:19—"They went out from us, but they were not of us . . . if they had been of us, they would no doubt have continued with us." True faith continues.

4. 1 John 5:5—"Who is he that overcometh the world, but he that believeth [lit., "continues to believe"] that Jesus is the Son of God?"

If a person's salvation is genuine, his faith in Christ will be continual. If the confession of sin that led to salvation was real, you will continue to confess your sin. The Christian is to continually admit the truth about himself and agree with what God says about his sin. The phrase "If we confess" indicates habitual action. The word "confess" means "to say the same thing." And if we admit the truth about our sin, we give evidence of being believers.

Forgiveness and cleansing come as a result of what Christ did on the cross. It comes only to those who prove they are saved through their continual belief and their confession of sins. Continual confession characterizes Christians.

d) The particulars

There can be varying degrees of thoroughness in confession among Christians. Some believers might confess their sins more frequently than others. There may be degrees in the fullness of repentance. But the same is true of faith. Some of us have greater faith than others. A man once said to Jesus, "Lord, I believe; help thou mine unbelief" (Mark 9:24). Christ spoke of faith the size of "a grain of mustard seed" (Luke 17:6). And God wants to expand our faith through His Word. Just as with faith, there are degrees of thoroughness in confession. There is full repentance and incomplete repentance. But just as faith has to be present for someone to be a Christian, confession has to be present to prove that someone is a believer. Let's look at what's involved in true confession.

Evidently our belief can outweigh our faith; this is not good.

(1) Sorrow over sin

One's sorrow over sin can't be superficial. Paul said that we must have a godly sorrow that "worketh repentance to salvation" (2 Cor. 7:10). True confession revolves around our sorrow over our sin.

(2) Repentance

Repentance means you stop what you are doing and do the opposite. True confession isn't just saying, "Lord, I'm sorry about what I did." True confession involves saying, "Lord, I'm sorry

54

about what I did, and I won't do it anymore." That's repentance. Go, + Sin No MorL—

? It's important for us to be honest with God about our sins. The blessing of God is attendant upon the confessing heart. If you are a Christian and you try to cover up your sin, you will feel the same way David did in Psalm 32. His vitality was sucked away as if a fervent summer heat were draining him, and his body ached from his groanings over his guilt (vv. 3-4). A true believer eventually confesses his sin. When you bottle up sin in yourself, you make yourself sick. Ill: Zach-Took it further with God + Man—

Confession is basically a detailed admission of your sin to God. The confessions that are in the Word of God show a true pouring out of the heart. If you have a superficial relationship with God, your confession will also be superficial. You will say something like, "Lord, I sinned again today, and You know it. There are many things I did; I don't have time to go into them all. Amen." You may admit you are a sinner, but you may be more of one than you confess to be. It is much more meaningful to plumb the depths of your heart and truly acknowledge your sinfulness to God. If you say to yourself, "I haven't done anything serious," then you are blind.

The Joy of Confession

Whether or not a believer confesses his sin, he is still in the fellowship, because fellowship with God can't be broken. We have been victimized by the English usage of the word *fellowship*, which today means "friendship, intimacy, or relationships between two people." That's not the meaning of the Greek work *koinōnia*, which means "partnership." You say, "But something does happen when a Christian sins." That's true. However, a sinning believer isn't out of the fellowship; he forfeits his joy. John said. "These things write we unto you, that your joy may be full" (1 John 1:4). When you sin, fellowship can't be broken because you are in the light, but you can foul up your life so that your joy is gone. There are many Christians who do that.

If you lose your joy, do you know how to get it back? in Psalm 51:12, David says to the Lord, "Restore unto me the joy of thy salvation." You get your joy back by confession. You don't need to get back into the fellowship because you are already there; you need to have your joy restored. When you sin, there is a sense of intimacy with God that is lost, and that can be defined as joy.

The third word we can use to characterize a Christian is:

3. Conquering (2:1a)

"My little children, these things write I unto you, that ye sin not."

a) The complacency

Christians do not have to sin. What liberty! Some people say, "Because I have Christian liberty, I can do anything I want." But do you know what Christian liberty really is? It's the freedom for the first time to do what's right. You never could do that before you became saved. Everything you did was wrong. John has a specific message in mind in 1 John 2:1, knowing that after reading chapter 1 someone might say to himself, "Since I will never be able to get rid of sin completely, and I have to continually confess my sinfulness, why should I bother trying to live a holy life? I am constantly being cleansed anyway, so I may as well do whatever I want. Since God loves to cleanse sin, I'll let Him enjoy Himself."

b) The command

To make sure no one responded that way, John said, "My little children, these things write I unto you, that ye sin not" (1 John 2:1). John was about ninety years old when he wrote that, so he could say, "My little children." I like his exhortation: "People, don't sin!" We don't need to do a word study on that statement; it's very clear. You say, "If I'm always going to be confessing sin and needing to be cleansed, isn't it a little ridiculous to say, 'Don't sin'?" No, because you don't have to sin. It may seem John was being contradictory, but he was emphasizing that within you is the power for victory. That's why I use the title *Conquering* for this section of our study. You can conquer sin.

(1) Romans 6:14—"For sin shall not have dominion over you." Sin has no power over a believer.

56

(2) Romans 8:13—"Mortify the deeds of the body." You can kill sin. That's something an unbeliever can't do. He neither acknowledges it, nor can he stop it. The Christian deals with sin and conquers it.

I believe spiritual maturity is the decreasing frequency of sin. As you grow in Christ, you sin less frequently. God would never say, "Don't sin," if you didn't have the resources to do so.

(3) 1 Corinthians 15:34—Paul said, "Awake to righteousness, and sin not." That's the same exhortation as the one John gave in 1 John 2:1.

(4) Ephesians 4:26—"Be ye angry, and sin not."

(5) Titus 2:11-12—"For the grace of God that bringeth salvation hath appeared to all men, teaching us that, denying ungodliness and wordly lusts, we should live soberly, righteously, and godly, in this present age." That's how we are to live. Don't sin.

Three things characterize the Christian: He is continually cleansed, he is continually confessing, and he is conquering sin.

III. THE DELIVERANCE (2:1b-2)

"And if any man sin, we have an advocate with the Father, Jesus Christ the righteous; and he is the propitiation for our sins, and not for ours only, but also for the sins of the whole world."

A. Christ the advocate

John said, "In case you do sin, there is someone who can cover it for you." The phrase "if any man sin" is an aorist subjunctive in the Greek text that refers to a single act of sin, not habitual sin. If a Christian commits a sin, he is cleansed. When we sin, Jesus Christ is our advocate. The word "advocate" is a translation of the Greek word *paraclētos*, the same word that is translated "Comforter" in John 15:26, where Christ referred to the Holy Spirit. *Paraclētos* means "a lawyer for the defense," or "someone called alongside to help." It is a beautiful concept.

Satan loves to accuse us whenever we sin. Revelation 12:10 says he accuses us before God day and night. When you sin, he says to God, "Look at him! He sinned!" Satan is the prosecutor, and Christ is the lawyer for the defense. His response to Satan's accusation is, "Father, that person's sin is taken care of. I bore it on My body; I took the penalty." Christ is the advocate for the defense. He is our supporter. Romans 8 says, "Who shall lay any thing to the charge of God's elect?" (v.33). Satan can't successfully accuse us. Christ has taken care of our sins. He is our helper and advocate. Nineteenth-century English poet Christina Rossetti wrote these words in her poem "Day and Night the Accuser Makes No Pause":

> Day and night the accuser makes no pause,
> Day and night protest the Righteous Laws.
> Good and evil witness to man's flaws;
> Man the culprit, man's the desperate cause
> Man midway to death's devouring jaws,
> And the worm that gnaws.

> Day and night our Jesus makes no pause,
> Pleads His own fulfillment of all laws,
> Veils with His perfections mortal flaws,
> Clears the culprit, pleads the desperate cause,
> Plucks the dead from death's devouring jaws,
> And the worm that gnaws.

Christ is our high priest, advocate, and defender. John called Him "Jesus Christ the righteous" (1 John 2:1). Only a righteous person can save us from all unrighteousness. Jesus is holy; He is the perfect sacrifice.

B. Christ the appeaser

1. For all believers

John said Christ is "the propitiation for our sins" (1 John 2:2). When we sin, He doesn't plead to the Father that we are innocent. He doesn't say, "That's OK; they are innocent, Father. Don't believe the devil." Rather, He says, "They are guilty. However, I have taken care of their sins." The Greek word for "propitiation" is *hilasmos*, and it appears in many forms in the New Testament. It refers to the appeasement of a god. When God's justice or love has been trampled upon, He must be appeased. When we sin, God becomes angry. He has holy antagonism toward evil. However, Christ's death paid for our sins, and thus He satisfied God's judgment on sin. He is the satisfaction for our sins. What He did on the cross satisfied God. How do we know that? Philippians 2 says that after Christ died on the cross, God exalted Him and gave Him a name above every name (v.9). Christ is our propitiation.

So, as Christians we are cleansed when we sin, and we continually agree with God that we are sinners. As a result, we can conquer sin. When we fail to conquer it, Jesus Christ is our advocate. He pleads our case. Even though we are guilty, He has satisfied the law's requirement for punishment.

2. For all the world

John said Christ "is the propitiation for our sins, and not for ours only, but also for the sins of the whole world." What Jesus did on the cross is applicable to any man who comes to Him. What an invitation!

Conclusion

If you are denying sin, you are being foolish. A person who denies sin is in the darkness. He deceives himself and defames the character of God. Why not own up to your sin and accept the perfect sacrifice that has already been given for it? You have nothing to lose. If you hide your sin now, God will uncover it, and you will pay for it throughout eternity. If you uncover your sin now, God will cover it in the blood of Jesus Christ. Listen to the invitation John gives. Don't deny sin and die in it. Be one of those who are characterized by continual confession, continual cleansing, and the ability to conquer sin.

Focusing on the Facts

1. What two options did Adam have when he sinned? Which one did he pick? What does Proverbs 28:13 say about such a choice (see p. 42)?

2. What does 1 Corinthians 4:5 say will happen someday? Explain what God will do with the sins of believers and unbelievers (see p. 43).

3. Against whom is sin, primarily (see p. 43)?

4. What is significant about the word "walk" in 1 John 1:7 (see p. 46)?

5. Describe the nature of the Christian's fellowship with God (see p. 47).

6. What does the blood that Christ shed on the cross symbolize (see p. 47)?

7. From how many of our sins has Christ's blood cleansed us? Support your answer with Scripture (see p. 49).

8. What is John 13:10 an illustration of (see p. 49)?

9. Does 1 John 1:9 say confession is a condition for cleansing? Explain (see pp. 49-50).

10. What does God promise to do for those who confess their sins (Prov. 28:13; see p. 50)?

11. How can God be just and at the same time forgive sin (see p. 50)?

12. The word translated "forgive" in 1 John 1:9 is in the aorist tense. What does that indicate (see p. 51)?

13. Describe some of the different perspectives on confessing sin. What does 1 John 1:9 really say about confessing sin (see pp. 52-53)?

14. Is belief in Christ a one-time thing? Use Scripture to support your answer (see p. 53).

15. If a person's salvation is genuine, his _____ will be _____ (see p. 54).

16. What is involved in true confession? Explain (see pp. 54-55).

17. Confession is basically a ___ ___ of your sin to God (see p. 55).

18. Does a believer's sin affect his position in the fellowship? What does a believer forfeit when he sins? How can he get that back (see pp. 55-56)?

19. Define Christian liberty. What did the apostle John think some people might say after reading 1 John 1? What did he say to make sure that didn't happen (see p. 56)?

20. What does Scripture say about the believer's ability to conquer sin (see p. 56)?

21. What is one way spiritual maturity can be defined (see p. 57)?

22. What does the word "advocate" (Gk., *paraclētos*) in 1 John 2:1 mean (see p. 57)?

23. What does Satan love to do whenever we sin? What is Christ's response (see pp. 57-58)?

24. Explain what John meant when he said Christ is "the propitiation for our sins" (1 John 2:2 see p. 58).

25. To whom does Christ's deed on the cross apply (see p. 59)?

Pondering the Principles

1. A person cannot have fellowship with God and habitually live in sin, because in God there "is no darkness at all" (1 John 1:5). According to Galatians 5:22-23; 1 Peter 4:7-16; and 2 Peter 1:3-7, what are some of the attitudes and actions Christians are to be

characterized by? Which are you strong in? Thank God for helping you in those areas. Are there some godly attitudes or actions that you have not been manifesting recently? Determine how you can change that. Can you think of other characteristics we should manifest as people of the light?

2. You may know someone who believes that a person has to be saved two or more times if he sins too much. Some people also believe that Christ's death does not cover all our sins at one time. A good verse to know when encountering such people is Hebrews 10:14: "For by one offering [Christ] has perfected for all time those who are sanctified" (NASB). Take time now to memorize that verse.

3. Read Ephesians 4:1—5:21 and answer the following questions: How does Paul contrast the lives of believers and unbelievers? Write down the characteristics in the life-styles of both. What specific exhortations does Paul give on how we should live?

4. It is important for us to be honest with God about our sins. Do you spend an adequate amount of time admitting your sins in detail to God when you pray? Do you express true penitence and humility over your sins? What can we gain by doing those things?

4
True Confession

Outline

Introduction
A. The Focus on Sin
B. The Facts About Confession
   1. Its endurance
      a) Continual confession
      b) Permanent forgiveness
   2. Its elements
      a) Agreement with God
      b) Repentance from sin

Lesson
I. A Right View of Sin
  A. Sin Deserves Judgment
  B. The Sinner Appeals for Mercy
  C. Sin Demands Cleansing
  D. The Sinner Accepts Full Responsibility
  E. Sin Proceeds from Human Nature
II. A Right View of God
  A. God's Holiness
  B. God's Power
  C. God's Chastisement
    1. Exemplified
    2. Expected
  D. God's Forgiveness
    1. Acknowledged by David
    2. Acknowledged by the prophets
III. A Right View of Self
  A. For the Sake of Sinners
  B. For the Sake of God
  C. For the Sake of the Saints

Introduction

Psalm 51 is a great psalm that is familiar to anyone who comes from a liturgical background. Many parts of Psalm 51 appear in the liturgy of the church. It's a powerful psalm, and its theme is true confession.

A. The Focus on Sin

The church is probably the only organization where people meet together regularly to describe themselves as miserable sinners. Some people say, "I don't go to church because there are so many hypocrites and sinners there." But the church is not a society of perfect people; it's like a hospital, and at least we recognize we are all sick. We also know where to find healing.

I suppose some people would say that we who go to church are preoccupied with sin because we always talk about it. That's true, but that's because the Bible discusses sin at length. How could it be any other way when the Bible chronicles human history and experience, which is dominated by sin? If God's Word deals with truth, it will deal with sin. We who love the Bible will also deal with sin. A man with any moral sense—especially a man who knows that God hates sin—will be unnerved over his sin. David was such a man, and that's why he wrote Psalm 51. That psalm bears the mark of deep inner guilt, and it presents the character of true confession. Today, the topic of confessing sin is discussed frequently, so it's important that we look at it from a biblical perspective.

B. The Facts About Confession

1. Its endurance

   a) Continual confession

   One characteristic of a Christian is that he continually confesses his sins. First John 1:9 literally reads, "If we are the ones confessing our sins, God is faithful and just to keep on forgiving us." A Christian continually confesses, and God continually forgives. The Christian deals with his sin regularly.

   b) Permanent forgiveness

   To confess your sins doesn't mean you beg for forgiveness. We don't need to beg for God's forgiveness because He has already forgiven us. When Jesus died on the cross, He bore all our sins in His body. I have no unforgiven sin in my life, and neither do you if you are a Christian. God's forgiveness was extended when Christ died on the cross. John said, "Your sins are forgiven you for His name's sake" (1 John 2:12). There is no such thing as an unforgiven sin in a believer's life. I remember an interview I heard on television some time ago where a Christian woman asked, "If I sin and the rapture takes place before I can ask for forgiveness, what will happen to me?" The answer was, "You will go to hell because your sin will have been unforgiven." That's not true. All your sins are forgiven at the cross.

2. Its elements

True confession has two elements.

a) Agreement with God

The word "confess" is the Greek word *homologeō*, which means "to say the same thing." To confess your sins is the same as agreeing with God that you are a sinner.

b) Repentance from sin

True confession involves repentance. You don't just say, "God, forgive me"; you say, "God, I've sinned. Thank you for already forgiving me. I want to turn from my sin." You haven't honestly confessed your sin until you've stopped doing it. Saying, "I'm sorry Lord: I confess my sin," at the same time you are continuing in your sin is not true confession. Paul writes in 2 Corinthians 7:8-10, "For though I made you sorry with a letter, I do not repent, though I did repent [i.e., I felt bad]; for I perceive that the same epistle hath made you sorry, though it were for but a season. Now I rejoice, not that ye were made sorry but that ye sorrowed to repentance. . . . For godly sorrow worketh repentance." True confession is exhibited by saying, "Lord, I have sinned, and I agree with Your estimate of me. I'm a sinner, and I want to turn from my sin." To just say, "Please forgive me," is superfluous. If I'm going to confess my sin, I must agree with God that I'm a sinner and see my sin the way He does. I also must turn from my sin; I can't just say, "I did it."

True confession involves a brokenness of heart that changes a person's behavior. As we look at Psalm 51, we will see the character of true confession, which involves a right view of three things: sin, God, and self. True confession will occur only when you see sin for what it is, God for who He is, and yourself for what you are.

The Sin Behind Psalm 51

King David was a ladies' man. When he wanted a woman, he took her—even to the point of taking someone else's wife on at least one occasion. When David was at the height of his power, he became infatuated with the wife of one of his military officers (2 Sam. 11:2-4). Her name was Bathsheba, and she became pregnant (v. 5). David decided to solve that problem by arranging for Bathsheba's husband to lead a suicide squad into the midst of a battle, thereby bringing about his death. Then conveniently forgetting his intrigue, he gave the man a military funeral and married his pregnant wife. However, David couldn't get rid of his guilt. He was convicted about his sin and couldn't get away from it. He felt its consequences for the rest of his life. He couldn't get his sin out of his heart or mind. Psalm 51 came as a result of anxiety it produced. In Psalm 51, he prayed for four things: Sin made him dirty, and he asked to be cleansed; guilt made him physically sick, and he asked to be healed; iniquity broke his friendship with God, and he asked for it to be restored. And most of all, he asked for pardon and mercy. Psalm 51 is a psalm of confession.

Lesson

I. A RIGHT VIEW OF SIN (vv. 1-5)

"Have mercy upon me, O God, according to thy loving-kindness; according unto the multitude of thy tender mercies blot out my transgressions. Wash me thoroughly from mine iniquity, and cleanse me from my sin. For I acknowledge my transgressions, and my sin is ever before me. Against thee, thee only, have I sinned, and done this evil in thy sight, that thou mightest be justified when thou speakest, and be clear when thou judgest. Behold, I was shaped in iniquity, and in sin did my mother conceive me."

In those verses, David states his view of sin. There are several features that I think are worthy of notice.

A. Sin Deserves Judgment (v. 1)

David begins Psalm 51 with these words: "Have mercy upon me, O God, according to thy loving-kindness; according unto the multitude of thy tender mercies blot out my transgressions." David's pleading for mercy was an admission that he did not deserve to be acquitted. He was saying, "Have mercy upon me, God! Please don't give me what I deserve." Sin deserves judgment. In true confession, we must recognize that we do not deserve to be forgiven. The only thing David could appeal for was mercy. A person who pleads for mercy is admitting that he is guilty. Here are some Scripture verses that give additional insight.

1. Psalm 103:10-11

   Verse 10 says, "[God] hath not dealt with us after our sins, nor rewarded us according to our iniquities." Aren't you glad about that? God hasn't given us what we deserve. Verse eleven continues, "For as the heavens are high above the earth, so great is his mercy toward them that fear him." Praise God for His mercy! David recognized that sin deserves judgment, and he asked God to spare him.

2. Psalm 130:3

   Here we read, "If thou, Lord, shouldest mark iniquities, O Lord, who shall stand?" The psalmist was saying, "Lord, if you gave people what they deserve for their sins, no one would survive!"

3. Ezra 9:13-14

   Ezra told the Israelites, "After all that is come upon us for our evil deeds, and for our great trespass, seeing that thou, our God, hast punished us less than our iniquities deserve, and hast given us such deliverance as this, should we again break thy commandments, and join in affinity with the people of these abominations?" He was saying, "After all the mercy God has shown us in the past, giving us less than our iniquities deserve, should we sin again? Should we tread on such mercy?"

   Notice that in the confessions we have looked at so far, sin deserved judgment. However, God's mercy stayed the hand of judgment.

4. Nehemiah 9:3

   Nehemiah 9 talks about a revival that the Israelites had.

They spent one-fourth of a day confessing their sins to God (v. 3). Then they pleaded for mercy. One of the things a Christian has to recognize is that he deserves judgment. True confession acknowledges that.

5. Job 11:6

    Job said, "Know, therefore, that God exacteth of thee less than thine iniquity deserveth." Isn't that beautiful? God requires less than your sin deserves. Sin deserves judgment; we deserve hell. But God, who is full of mercy, forgives those of us who are Christians and covers our sins with the blood that Jesus Christ shed at the cross. Job 11:6 is a marvelous promise. And yet we don't deserve God's mercy.

B. The Sinner Appeals for Mercy (v. 1)

    There is nothing for a Christian to appeal for but mercy. Throughout the book of Romans, the apostle Paul essentially says, "Our only appeal is to grace and mercy." Romans 11:32 says, "God hath concluded them all in unbelief, that he might have mercy upon all." God is eager to extend His mercy. Ephesians 2 says, "God, who is rich in mercy, for his great love with which he loved us, even when we were dead in sins, hath made us alive together with Christ. . . . For by grace are ye saved, through faith; and that not of yourselves, it is the gift of God—not of works, lest any man should boast" (vv. 4-5, 8-9). Our salvation comes from God's mercy. The sinner has to appeal for mercy; there is no other appeal he can make. That's exactly what David did in Psalm 51. He cried, "O God . . . according unto the multitudes of thy tender mercies blot out my transgressions" (v. 1).

C. Sin Demands Cleansing (v. 2)

    Habakkuk said God is "of purer eyes than to behold evil, and canst not look on iniquity" (1:13). God demands that sin be cleansed. In Psalm 51:2, David says, "Wash me thoroughly from mine iniquity, and cleanse me from my sin." "Wash me" refers to a cleanser used on a foul garment. The Hebrew word used for "sin" in that verse was a general word that referred to every kind of uncleanness and evil. David wanted God to wash sin out of his life and purify him. When sin leaves a deep stain, only total cleansing can suffice.

    The forgiveness that Christians have in Christ is aptly illustrated in John 13. Jesus says to Peter in verse 10, "He that is washed needeth not except to wash his feet, but is entirely clean; and ye are clean, but not all of you." (The one who wasn't clean was Judas.) Jesus was saying, "Peter, once you've had a bath and continue in life, you don't need another bath; you just need to get your feet washed off regularly." Christ gave us a bath when He died on the cross. He totally cleansed us, and now He washes off our feet to remove the dust that we gather as we walk in the world. A Christian doesn't need to get saved twice; he just needs to have the dirt of the world cleansed off his feet day by day. That's the work of the Lord Jesus Christ. He is still righteous and continually cleansing us from all sin. I'm so glad for His forgiveness and cleansing! *Much sin is Blamed on others in our lives - "Adam said," "The Woman you gave me"*

D. The Sinner Accepts Full Responsibility (vv. 3-4)

What David says in Psalm 51:3 is very important: "For I acknowledge my transgressions, and my sin is ever before me." He didn't blame anyone else for his sin; he blamed himself. In Joshua 7:19, Joshua says to a man named Achan, "My son, give, I pray thee, glory to the Lord God of Israel, and make confession unto him." God is honored when you take responsibility for your sin. Some people blame their sins on others. For example, Adam blamed God for his sin. When God asked Adam why he sinned, Adam essentially responded, "It's Your fault because of the woman you gave me" (Gen. 3:11-12). To an extent, he was also blaming Eve. There are people who blame Satan for what they do. They say, "The devil made me do it." However, David blamed himself. The prodigal son in Luke 15 said to his father, "I have sinned against heaven, and in thy sight" (v. 21).

True confession involves accepting full liability for sin. When you sin, you should say, "Lord, I know I did that." Don't say things like, "Lord, why did you allow me to get into this situation? You are sovereign; why did this happen if you don't want me to get into trouble? You know I'm weak in that area." When a person does that, he impugns what God says about sin. He violates God's holiness and sins doubly. Don't beg off your sins. I like what one of the thieves crucified with Christ said to the other thief: "We, indeed, [suffer] justly; for we receive the due reward of our deeds. But this man hath done nothing amiss" (Luke 23:41). That thief accepted responsibility for his sin. Confession demands responsibility. When David said in Psalm 51:4, "Against thee, thee only, have I sinned, and done this evil in thy sight," he was saying, "God, I exonerate You. I myself have sinned, and I've done

it against You. I don't hold You responsible; this is my fault."
A Christian who takes the responsibility for his own sin is
mature.

E. Sin Proceeds from Human Nature (v. 5)

Here David said, "Behold, I was shaped in iniquity, and in
sin did my mother conceive me." The Bible teaches that life
begins at conception. At that moment, the sin principle is
operative. David admitted that when he wrote Psalm 51:5.
You say, "Do you believe in the total depravity of man?
Absolutely. I believe in congenital depravity—that sin is
passed on from generation to generation from the time of
conception. Psalm 58:3 says, "The wicked are estranged from
the womb; they go astray as soon as they are born." Man's
pattern of depravity is mentioned even further back in the
Bible. Genesis 8:21 says, "The imagination of man's heart is
evil from his youth." From the very beginning, man has been
evil. In Job 14:4 we read, "Who can bring a clean thing out of
an unclean? Not one." No one can do that.

So, in true confession, we must recognize several things about
sin: it deserves judgment, it demands cleansing, it accepts full
responsibility, and it proceeds from human nature. True confession also brings a sinner to appeal for mercy. There are many
people who aren't willing to recognize those things. They don't
like to hear that they are sinners. They are like the Jews Paul
addressed in Romans 2-3, who were proud of their supposed
spirituality. They thought they were holy, but Paul said to them,
"Thy hardness and impenitent heart treasurest up unto thyself
wrath against the day of wrath and revelation of the righteous
judgment of God" (2:5). He said that God is going to judge the
secret things of a man's heart (2:16) and that they would be
exposed. We must all recognize that we are born sinners. That's
where true confession starts.

II. A RIGHT VIEW OF GOD (vv. 6-12)

"Behold, thou desirest truth in the inward parts, and in the
hidden part thou shalt make me know wisdom. Purge me with
hyssop, and I shall be clean; wash me, and I shall be whiter than
snow. Make me hear joy and gladness, that the bones which thou
hast broken may rejoice. Hide thy face from my sins, and blot out
all mine iniquities. Create in me a clean heart, O God, and renew
a right spirit within me. Cast me not away from thy presence,
and take not thy holy Spirit from me. Restore unto me the joy of

thy salvation, and uphold me with a willing spirit."

A. God's Holiness (v. 6)

David said, "Behold, thou desirest truth in the inward parts, and in the hidden part thou shalt make me know wisdom." God is not concerned solely about external behavior; He is concerned with what is going on inside us. David said that God desires truth on the inside. That speaks of true holiness. Considering the context of David's words, he was saying, "God, I know You don't desire the processes of exterior ceremonial purification that every Jew is used to. I know that isn't what You are after. What You want is truth on the inside." God is holy. True confession involves recognizing that He doesn't care about how often you go to church or how many Christian books you have. He is concerned about the inside. Man looks at the outward appearance, but God looks at the heart (1 Sam. 16:7). So the first thing David recognizes as he looks at God is that the Lord is concerned with the inside of man.

A person can play games on the outside and go through religious folderol, but that doesn't get to the issue. True confession involves taking into account that God, who is absolutely holy, demands holiness in our lives. James 4:8 says, "Draw near to God, and he will draw near to you. Cleanse your hands, ye sinners; and purify your hearts." Clean the inside. Get to the real issue. Don't just deal with your sin externally; deal with the dirt in your heart that made you do what you did. David knew God wasn't as concerned with the outside as He was with the inside, for the latter determines our external behavior.

B. God's Power (vv. 7, 10)

At the beginning verse 7, David says, "Purge me with hyssop, and I will be clean." Hyssop was a bush, and it was used to apply blood and water in purification ceremonies (Ex. 12:22; Heb. 9:19-20). David had confidence in the power of God. He said, "If You purge me, I will be clean." At the end of verse 7, he continues, "Wash me, and I shall be whiter than snow." At the beginning of verse 8 David acknowledges that God could make him "hear joy and gladness." David recognized not just God's holiness, but also His power. He knew the Lord could change Him. That's important, because some Christians don't believe God can change their sinful habits. I believe He can.

Sometimes people get to the point where they wonder if God has the power to help them because they repeatedly fall into sin. They say, "God, can't you help me?" Psalm 51:7 is an encouragement to us that God *can* purge and cleanse us. But you have to come to Him with a broken heart, just as David did.

In verse 10 David says, "Create in me a clean heart, O God, and renew a right spirit within me." He was saying, "Renew me, Lord; start from scratch. I want more than just cleansing; I want a new heart." True confession involves recognizing that God can change and cleanse you. I'm amazed at how many people don't really trust God in that area of their lives.

C. God's Chastisement (vv. 8, 12)

    1. Exemplified

        David says in verse 8, "Make me hear joy and gladness, that the bones which thou hast broken may rejoice." When he said that, he had in mind something that shepherds did with wayward sheep. A shepherd took such a sheep and broke one of its legs. Then he would set the leg and carry the animal until it got better. During that time, the sheep would grow to love the shepherd. When the sheep was well enough to walk on its own again, it no longer ran off. Instead, it followed the shepherd everywhere. So David was saying, "Lord, I've had my legs broken. I'm ready to follow You." The sin David committed with Bathsheba was a great catalyst that led to his living a holier life. It brought about a personal reformation.

    2. Expected

        We need to recognize that we deserve chastisement. We also need to realize that God's mercy doesn't necessarily eliminate chastisement. God tells us, "I love you, I forgive you, and this is what I'm going to do to you." I like what David says in Psalm 51:8. He didn't want to ignore the conviction he was experiencing; he wanted active joy. He didn't say, "God, help me just to endure this situation. I want to be happy." He said, "I got what I deserved, and I've repented of my sin. Now I want to be joyous again." Then he says in verse 12, "Restore unto me the joy of thy salvation, and uphold me with a willing spirit."

        Do you see what chastisement is to do in your life? When

you sin, God chastises you because he wants to bring you to the place where you will say, "God, I've got the message. You broke my leg; now I want my joy and gladness back."

One who has a right view of God recognizes His holiness. The Lord expects us to have inward holiness. His power can change your life. He can help you change your sinful habits. We must recognize that He chastises us to conform us to Himself. He does that to make us repent and desire restoration.

D. God's Forgiveness (vv. 9, 11)

1. Acknowledged by David

David said, "Hide thy face from my sins, and blot out all mine iniquities. . . . Cast me not away from thy presence, and take not thy holy Spirit from me" (vv. 9-11). David believed that God pardoned sin. He wouldn't have asked Him to do so if he didn't. He said, "Lord, I know you are a forgiving God."

2. Acknowledged by the prophets

The prophets gave us great words on God's forgiving character. In Isaiah 43:25 God says, "I, even I, am he who blotteth out thy transgressions for mine own sake, and will not remember thy sins." You say, "He forgives us for His sake and not ours? Why is that?" So that you may know He is a merciful God. His nature is revealed through His forgiveness of our sins. I love what Micah 7:18-19 says about God's forgiveness: "Who is a God like unto thee, who pardoneth iniquity, and passeth by the transgression of the remnant of his heritage? He retaineth not his anger forever, because he delighteth in mercy. He will turn again; he will have compassion on us; he will subdue our iniquities; and thou wilt cast all their sins into the depths of the sea."

Notice that in Psalm 51:11 David says, "Take not thy holy Spirit from me." That is a good indication that the Old Testament saints did not have the permanent indwelling of the Spirit. That's something all Christians possess now; there is no statement in the New Testament that parallels Psalm 51:11. The Holy Spirit is ours as the guarantee of our heritage in Christ (Eph. 1:13-14).

III. A RIGHT VIEW OF SELF (vv. 13-19)

We need to constantly say to ourselves, "I must be holy. I must live for God." There are three reasons for that.

A. For the Sake of Sinners (vv. 13-15)

When David's joy was restored by God (v. 12), he said to the Lord, "Then will I teach transgressors thy ways, and sinners shall be converted unto thee" (v. 13). David knew he needed to be holy for the sake of sinners. He knew he wasn't any good to God as a witness if he wasn't pure. First Peter 2:9 says we are "an holy nation, a people of his own, that ye should show forth the praises of him." When sin is eating away at you and making you feel gulity, you won't be an effective witness for Christ.

Psalm 51:14 continues, "Deliver me from bloodguiltiness, O God, thou God of my salvation, and my tongue shall sing aloud of thy righteousness." Where there is guilt, there will be an inability to witness to God's righteousness. Then in verse 15 David says "O Lord, open thou my lips, and my mouth shall show forth thy praise." David couldn't open his mouth for the sake of God because he had no sense of forgiveness until he confessed his sin with Bathsheba. He had no sense of holiness. Guilt will shut your mouth too. I'm sure there are many Christians who cannot declare the righteousness of God because of their vile, unrighteous lives. So you must be holy for the sake of sinners, that they might be converted.

B. For the Sake of God (vv. 16-17)

Here David says, "Thou desirest not sacrifice, else would I give it; thou delightest not in burnt offering. The sacrifices of God are a broken spirit; a broken and contrite heart, O God, thou wilt not despise." He was saying to God, "I must be holy because that pleases You. I know You're not concerned with external ceremonies, but with internal holiness." Do you want to bring joy to God? We are more than willing to take the joy that He gives us. But do you want to make God happy? Be holy. God desires a heart broken over sin. That pleases Him.

C. For the Sake of the Saints (vv. 18-19)

In closing Psalm 51, David says, "Do good in thy good pleasure unto Zion; build thou the walls of Jerusalem. Then shalt thou be pleased with the sacrifices of righteousness, with burnt offering and whole burnt offering; then shall they offer bullocks upon thine altar." There David was praying for others. He was saying, "God, rebuild Jerusalem and bring everyone back to righteousness." By the time David wrote verse 18, he was back on holy ground again—he was cleansed from his sin and forgiven—and praying for others.

You can't pray to God unless there is purity in your life. A classic illustration of that appears in 1 Peter 3: "Husbands, dwell with [your wives] according to knowledge, giving honor unto the wife, as unto the weaker vessel, and as being heirs together of the grace of life, that your prayers be not hindered" (v. 7). If things aren't right between a husband and his wife, his prayers are hindered. Where there is unholiness, prayer is hindered. David recognized that and said, "Lord, I have to confess my sin." He sets a pattern for us in Psalm 51 that considers the ministry we have to other people. Psalm 66:18 says, "If I regard iniquity in my heart, the Lord will not hear me."

True confession involves a right view of sin, God, and self. We must be holy for the sake of sinners, God, and other saints. We must see that sin deserves judgment and that all we can do is appeal for mercy. Do you know what gives us the boldness to do that? The knowledge that God is willing to pardon sin. How do we know He will do that? Because He said He would, and He has proved His faithfulness to do so.

Focusing on the Facts

1. Why is the church so concerned about sin (see p. 64)?
2. True confession involves a _____of heart that changes a person's _____(see p. 65).
3. What four things did David pray for in Psalm 51 (see p. 66)?
4. What does the fact that David pleaded for mercy prove about him (see p. 67)?
5. What was the psalmist saying in Psalm 130:3? What was Ezra saying to the Israelites in Ezra 9:13-14 (see p. 67)?
6. What is the only thing a sinner can appeal for (see p. 68)?
7. What does Habakkuk 1:13 say about God and sin? What does God demand of sin (see p. 68)?
8. God is _____when you take responsibility for your sin (Josh. 7:19; see p. 69).

9. Give examples of how people avoid taking responsibility for their sins. What is the result of doing that (see p. 69)?

10. Give scriptural support for the fact that sin proceeds from human nature (see p. 70).

11. What is God concerned about, according to Psalm 51:6? Explain (see p. 71).

12. What did David know God was capable of doing (Ps. 51:7, 10; see p. 71)?

13. What picture did David have in mind when he said, "Make me hear joy and gladness, that the bones which thou hast broken may rejoice" (Ps. 51:8; see p. 72)?

14. Does God's mercy eliminate any chastisement in our lives? Explain (see p. 72).

15. What does Psalm 51:9, 11 say about God? What does Micah 7:18-19 say about God's forgiveness (see p. 73)?

16. What did David say would happen when God restored the joy of salvation to him (Ps. 51:13)? Why is it important for us to be holy for the sake of others (see pp. 74)?

17. According to Psalm 51:16-17, what does God desire? How can we bring joy to Him (see p. 74)?

18. What happens to your prayers if there is sin in your life? Use Scripture to support your answer (see p. 75).

19. What gives believers the boldness to appeal to God for mercy? How do we know He will have mercy (see p. 75)?

Pondering the Principles

1. Some people say that Christians are obsessed with sin. Since sin is ingrained in man's nature and the Bible deals extensively with it, Christians have good reason to talk about it. What would happen to the church if believers ignored what God said about sin? Is it possible to witness without addressing the issue of sin? How would unbelievers perceive God if Christians didn't say that sin demands judgment? What other possible consequences could there be if believers ignored the issue of sin?

2. What do Romans 3:23 and 5:12 say about man? What do Psalm 51:5 and Romans 7:19-25 say about the nature of man? How should knowing that influence the way you live? According to Hebrews 12:1, what can sin do to us? Determine how to keep that from happening.

3. Answer the questions in the section below that applies to you:

a. You may have read this book knowing you are not a Christian, or you may have thought you were saved but found out that you never truly repented of your sins when you professed Christ as Savior and Lord. God is holy, and He demands that all who live in His kingdom be holy. Are you willing to give up attitudes, actions, and things in your thought life that offend God? The Bible clearly teaches that sinners deserve judgment. The Bible also says that God is "not willing that any should perish, but that all should come to repentance" (2 Pet. 3:9). God has the power to cleanse sinners, and He is willing to forgive anyone who confesses his sins. If you desire to turn from your sins, take time now to acknowledge your sinfulness to God. Ask Him to cleanse you, knowing that Christ died on the cross to pay the penalty for your sins. Put your trust in Him alone for eternal life. Then find a good Bible-teaching church and begin studying the Bible, for it teaches us about God and tells us how to live the Christian life.

b. If you have already received Christ as your Savior and Lord, take some time to meditate on the following questions:

1) Do you take sin seriously? Do you seek to be holy as God is holy? Discuss some good ways to cultivate holiness in your life.

2) Do you trust that God can cleanse you of your sins? If you are committing a particular sin repeatedly, have you considered that it may be because you don't hate that sin enough?

3) How well do you receive chastisement from God? How does chastisement help us?

4) How grateful are you for God's forgiveness of your sins? Do you express your gratitude to Him frequently?

Scripture Index

Moody Press, a ministry of the Moody Bible Institute, is designed for education, evangelization, and edification. If we may assist you in knowing more about Christ and the Christian life, please write us without obligation: Moody Press, c/o MLM, Chicago, Illinois 60610.